Mistress Ethics

ALSO AVAILABLE FROM BLOOMSBURY

The Future is Feminine: Capitalism and the Masculine Disorder,
Ciara Cremin
A Feminist Mythology, Chiara Bottici
Anarchafeminism, Chiara Bottici
The Feminist Uncanny in Theory and Art Practice,
Alexandra M. Kokoli

Mistress Ethics

On the Virtues of Sexual Kindness

VICTORIA BROOKS

BLOOMSBURY ACADEMIC
LONDON • NEW YORK • OXFORD • NEW DELHI • SYDNEY

BLOOMSBURY ACADEMIC
Bloomsbury Publishing Plc
50 Bedford Square, London, WC1B 3DP, UK
1385 Broadway, New York, NY 10018, USA
29 Earlsfort Terrace, Dublin 2, Ireland

BLOOMSBURY, BLOOMSBURY ACADEMIC and the Diana logo are
trademarks of Bloomsbury Publishing Plc

First published in Great Britain 2022

Cover design by Jade Barnett
Cover image © Gray Cat / Shutterstock

A catalogue record for this book is available from the British Library.

Library of Congress Cataloging-in-Publication Data
Names: Brooks, Victoria, author.
Title: Mistress ethics : on the virtues of sexual kindness / Victoria Brooks.
Description: London ; New York : Bloomsbury Academic, 2022. |
Includes bibliographical references and index.
Identifiers: LCCN 2021030306 (print) | LCCN 2021030307 (ebook) |
ISBN 9781350195738 (pb) | ISBN 9781350195721 (hb) |
ISBN 9781350195745 (epdf) | ISBN 9781350195752 (ebook)
Subjects: LCSH: Mistresses–History. | Sexual ethics–History, | Marriage–History.
Classification: LCC HQ806 .B75 2022 (print) | LCC HQ806 (ebook) |
DDC 306.73/609–dc23
LC record available at https://lccn.loc.gov/2021030306
LC ebook record available at https://lccn.loc.gov/2021030307

ISBN: HB: 978-1-3501-9572-1
         PB: 978-1-3501-9573-8
         ePDF: 978-1-3501-9574-5
         eBook: 978-1-3501-9575-2

Typeset by Integra Software Services Pvt. Ltd.
Printed and bound in Great Britain

To find out more about our authors and books visit www.bloomsbury.com
and sign up for our newsletters.

To Mistresses of all kinds, everywhere, past, present and future.

At night too, she puzzled the mystery of her desperate need of kindness. As other girls prayed for handsomeness in a lover, or for wealth, or for power, or for poetry, she had prayed fervently: let him be kind.

~ *Anaïs Nin,* A Spy in the House of Love

CONTENTS

ACKNOWLEDGEMENTS

This is the book I have always wanted to write, and I thank Liza Thompson and Lucy Russell at Bloomsbury for giving me the opportunity to do so, and for their support and enthusiasm. I would like to thank my loving friends, who offer boundless gifts of humour, kindness and support: in particular, Marc Mason (who kindly read and commented on drafts of this book), Matthew Jay, Wing-Yan Cheung, Simon Flacks, Naomi Creutzfeldt, Manvir Grewal, Andreas Philippopoulos-Mihalopoulos, Danilo Mandic, David Turner, Tom Moore and Simon Avery. I would like to thank Simon Avery in particular for casting his expert literary eye over drafts of various chapters, providing generous comments, introducing me to Jane Eyre and Marie Curie, and always being willing to talk excitedly about Mistresses and books. Thank you to Swastee Ranjan for her endless support of my work and for her exquisite feedback. Thank you also to Andy West for reading and commenting on drafts, and for encouraging my writing. I also thank the incredible community of thinkers and writers that I am honoured to be a part of and who offer strength and inspiration. In particular I would like to thank Meg-John Barker, Stoya, Lucie Fielding, Susan Finlay, Hannah Camplin, Alex Dymock, Alex Aldridge, Laurent de Sutter and Anna Chronopoulou for their support and inspiration. Thank you also to H and Matt Smith for the warm, kind and intellectually fierce seminar you arranged to discuss my work. The ideas we talked about, and the energy you gifted, have been crucial to this book. Thank you also to my partner, Roland Dannreuther, for your endless love and sexual kindness – although I am your wife, I am first and always your Mistress. Thank you to the queer community who have welcomed me and my proud bisexuality with open arms. Thank you to Dotty, my whippet, whose gifts defy words and are beyond human categorization. A special thank you to ELOP, who empowered me to start healing. Thank you to every Mistress there has been; is, and will be – I am standing and will always be standing on your shoulders. You are my heroes, and your stories are my philosophy. Sexual kindness, always.

PROLOGUE

It's hard to find stories written by Mistresses. There are so many about her but few *by* her. This book is a rare find: about Mistresses, and by a Mistress. This book is a celebration of her scandals, the virtues of the Mistress's superpower of sexual kindness, and of the extraordinary sexual kindness that a Mistress expresses for the world. It is *extra-*extraordinary that she has this superpower, given what we, our jealous laws, philosophies and romantic moralities, have done to her. The ranks of power double down to keep their Mistresses a secret, and for good reason. Even aspects of the stories of famous Mistresses such as Marilyn Monroe and Simone De Beauvoir have been hidden by the power that keeps Mistresses. Power does not want its Mistresses and their stories to be revealed, lest those in power are found responsible for the harm caused to her for centuries. What is concerning is that this harm is not just to the Mistress but to us all, since within her relationships is the possibility of revolution. There's a story that has been kept secret from us and it lies with the Mistress, in her bed. If we're lucky, and if we're kind, she might just let us in, to lie beside her and listen.

Her sexual kindness is revolutionary and could overturn the way that our sexual rules and assumptions oppress women of all kinds, from the most conventional to the most radical and proud queers, witches, splendid sluts and perverts. Her sexual kindness can tear apart the foundations of relationships as we know, understand and live them. Her story shows us the weaknesses in the structures we hold dear and transforms them with her pleasures, and teaches them with her traumas. In knowing the Mistress's suffering and her joy, we can know our own – this is the gift that is her sexual kindness.

Her relationships are always conducted on ethically shaky ground, and are usually undisclosed. She finds herself outside of the moral codes of monogamous and even polyamorous relationships, so there's no road map for her to follow towards ethical sex. She's even excluded from the most sex-positive ethical formulations. Her sexual kindness therefore adds an essential dimension to sex-positive ethics – She's much more than an Ethical Slut.[1] Her kindness reaches beyond conventional understandings of kindness, and because she's both an outsider and insider to our marriages, she has a unique power to make and destroy our worlds – and she knows it.

The Mistress is often a woman. References to women in this book are intended to include all women, and all people who identify as Mistresses. As a cis woman, I cannot speak from trans experience, but my hope is that this book will empower all kinds of people who are, or have been or desire to be Mistresses to write and talk about their experiences.

The Mistress is someone who's in a relationship with one (or perhaps both) of two partners who are married or in a long-term relationship which is, or is (at least overtly) understood by the partners in that relationship as, monogamous. She's often in a relationship that is undisclosed to the person who is married to her lover, and often undisclosed to the world, apart from, perhaps, a few trusted people. This lack of privilege to disclose her relationship is important and is part of what makes a Mistress. It's what takes her beyond an Ethical Slut and makes her a sexual kindness revolutionary.

This book is not only by and about Mistresses but it's *for* them, and it's about time. She enflames us because of her secrets. She arouses us – sexually, intellectually, morally, ethically, legally – and we punish her for it. She's considered a controversial figure and one who's at once feared and judged. Her legend is mired in mystery, myth and fantasy, yet we do not hear her story. This book is a chance to hold and create space for her. It's a room and book of her own. Often she's silenced because of the fear of her superpower, since it threatens to destroy the clarity of our sense of right and wrong. This is a sense that takes root in every part of our bodies. Yet, this is a sense that does not necessarily belong to us; rather, it's been made by laws, rules and society – things we thought were outside of us. Sexual kindness threatens to overthrow it all.

As we stand face to face with the Mistress, we're provoked, disgusted, titillated and frightened. The Mistress is an outsider, a sexual, loving, romantic alien, and within her is the passage to another, different, future. I'm going to try and bring us towards this future by delving into her world. Be warned, though, that it's not always a pretty place. Revolution is not borne of easy circumstances. You will see another side to love, and find your place in it too; and this can be hard to stomach.

This book tells the stories of many Mistresses, including the story of the author of this book. All of these stories are connected to other stories, untold and invisible and which paint and sculpt the figure that this book is dedicated to understanding. In telling these stories, my aim is to access and understand sexual kindness and how we can bring it into our lives – whether or not we are Mistresses or have Mistresses in our lives. My hope is that through understanding the Mistress, we might become sexually kinder to one another. I hope that through her, our aim as a society might switch, from being a sexual 'court', which appoints itself the judge of sex and desire in accordance with laws such as fidelity, censorship and conformity, to being a kinder society able to have better sex. The key component of this is to follow the Mistress, as a person uniquely positioned, to understand how the structures we have built and uphold harm our sexual lives. There will be elements that we might not wish to let go, things that bring us, or some of us, pleasure. Don't worry – the Mistress will tell us about those, too.

Mistress Ethics will take us beyond the choice between right and wrong. Perhaps we might meet the Mistress there, in this unchartered field, a non-judgemental space. Be prepared though – if I know her well enough, she might well be having sex with someone's wife in the tall spring grass of that luscious meadow.

This book, like the Mistress, targets the big structures that we're told we should never challenge. I'll reciprocate the gift that the Mistress gives by not being squeamish, and by telling her stories as unapologetically as she lives them, replete with flesh, fluids and fantasies, lubrications and menstrual blood, pregnancies and cervical mucous, traumas and perverse pleasures. Her kind of kindness is not clean and sensible, but is full of rage, slick with sex and embedded fully within the erotic. Hers is a s*exual* kindness, after all.

The Mistress who writes this book knows too that the ways in which marginalization and oppression reach us are vast and overwhelming, and that she writes it from her own location among these, as a white working-class queer cis woman. While I use my own experience and the experiences of others to build this *one* road map for accessing and developing the potentials of sexual kindness, there must be many others. To fully build and understand *Mistress Ethics*, stories that have not been told by Black women and women of colour, especially queer and trans Black women and women of colour, must be told.

Let's begin and let's take ourselves a Mistress. Let's have her in mind. Please do this for me now, if you will. Try to not only see her but become her. Make her in your own image, but let that image change as she goes through the adventures this book takes her through, and as she meets other Mistresses. Each chapter of this book will close with a series of bullet points and a fictional extract of a story. The bullet points are designed to show you an aspect of the Mistress's world that you might find surprising and which will also invite a kind of judgement. My hope is that by the end of this book, your perspective on these points might change. Each fictional extract is told to draw you into the world of the Mistress, so that you join her as protagonist, and through storytelling experience her suffering and her joy. Both of these are important if we are to develop a new ethical thinking. We must begin with her, and her body, rather than with what law and morality have required us to believe. This is how we will understand the virtues of sexual kindness, by practicing it ourselves. The first step is to listen.

Story Part I: Our Mistress

The cheap identikit hotel room stinks of sex. A royal-blue carpet matches a polyester bed-runner, which is now screwed up beside the bed. There must be many of these useless adornments suffering the same fate. It could be that our Mistress and her lover have stayed in this exact room before. It's hard to tell since the building itself is made to be anonymous, secret. The hotel room door has, just this second, slid shut, with a heavy slipping sound, and then… *click*. Our Mistress is sat on the edge of the bed. In the room's aggressive silence, she stares blankly at the bed runner. This is the moment she dreads, when her lover leaves, after spending the day with her. She inhales. She exhales.

The thought occurs to our Mistress that her lover's wife's sense of conjoined home is clear. Their home is right there, surrounding her; she and her husband come and go easily. His wife doesn't have to ensure she has enough money in her account in order to book a hotel room (these rooms are surprisingly expensive). She also doesn't have to feel the awkward shame of asking her lover for money. Our Mistress isn't sure why, but she's scared to ask her lover for help with the hotel room bill. Her lover's wife can rely on him returning home and she can be sure that this home will be full of… something. At least she's in the right. Our Mistress, however, is always on the wrong side. She's sure that she herself is wrong, and yet how can this be, since she's in love. Her lover tells her he loves her too, and he sure does show it. She remembers times when he just couldn't help himself – he's sometimes so overwhelmed with passion; she has no space to even think about what she wants. He tells her that without her, he'd die. This is real love.

Our Mistress doesn't feel like she has the strength to get up and shower today, but she must. It's check-out time soon. Our Mistress doesn't always feel so low. Sometimes, she smiles. Sometimes, her being is light with love and laughter, happy to ignore the silence; grateful for it, even. Occasions of feeling low sometimes didn't drown out her memories of laughing with her lover, while they rehearsed a possible shared future.

In *these* times, bright, clear images appear in our Mistress's mind, of the airy living room and overgrown kitchen garden that they will have, when he leaves his wife. She sometimes even dared to imagine the face of their child to come. There would be no safe suffocation in their home: the kind of conditional freedom our Mistress imagined her lover's wife to experience, but only space and lightness.

She didn't have this feeling today. She hung her head and let tears fall towards that tired and used bed-runner. How many trysts like hers and her lover's had it observed? She remembered what she read in an interview with Gillian Anderson, her bisexual icon, that Gillian thought it was a 'daily choice' to remain with someone. She wondered if she was entitled to make that choice, since she could hardly describe her relationship with her lover as 'daily'. They shared no day-to-day patterns. He couldn't even stay the night with her. Was she even 'with' him? What was she entitled to demand in this relationship, given that she's, from the start, in the wrong? If you're wrong, do you have rights? Can you question anything? Our Mistress didn't know if her lover wanted her to be faithful to him. She hoped so. He was the kind of man that probably assumed it. A thought caught in the throat of her mind – she wondered if he was faithful to her. In what box did she go when he had sex with his wife.

Our Mistress wasn't even sure if jealousy was what caused the thought to catch. She thought of her lover's wife and felt a warmth. Could it be an abstract jealousy that couldn't quite lock onto an object? Or, maybe, it was an as yet directionless feeling, perhaps even desire. Our Mistress felt that, soon, she might eventually be able to rise from the bedside, and re-construct herself into a presentable person. She'd then walk outside and check out of the hotel and walk towards the station. She felt starved, today. She wasn't sure of what. She only knew that if a stranger were to touch her kindly, or say a kind word, she'd shatter.

1

What is sexual kindness?

From Grand Central Station to new worlds

Elizabeth Smart is a superhero. Her prose poetry book *By Grand Central Station I Sat Down and Wept* is a semi-fictional account of Smart's eighteen-year affair with the married poet George Barker, with whom she had four children (although in the novel these pregnancies are distilled as one). My copy is on my desk, looking at me accusingly, as I begin to write. It is a rare piece of writing, remarkable for its time, in that Barker is barely described and we hear a story entirely from a Mistress. My copy has been inscribed with a poem from a married lover, from whom this book was a gift at the start of a toxic and abusive affair. The book is radical and free, but this was an unkind gift, since it was prophetic. Save for the four children and the length of the affair, this lover of mine was, in all but name, George Barker, and I, Smart. And I too, sat at many a station and wept. Not at stations as grand as *Grand Central*, but still. As I will soon make clear in this book, Smart is an archetypal Mistress. This is because she gives and gives, and for that, she is punished by the guardians of law and society (both actual and self-appointed): 'They eye me. They bore a hole in my wedding finger because it is bare.'[1] She is also punished by her lover who leaves her pregnant, and remains with his wife. So, through all this, what is it that keeps her surviving, fighting and writing?

Smart shows us that as a Mistress, one does not receive kindness from the world. The kindness that she needed was from both her lover and from those she encountered. She needed them to see her in the fullness of her humanity and sexuality, outside of the structures that would give her virtue. She needed them to see her not as a 'non-wife,' not as a friend, but in her glory as a powerful outsider, with traumas often thought of as deserved, and joys that are not. As a Mistress, she must not be acknowledged as deserving such humanity, nor indeed as giving it, since then the world might be required to revise some deeply treasured beliefs about men, monogamy, marriage and power. Perhaps even more fearfully, the world might see what it does to Mistresses, while also seeing the beauty and potential of their desire and sexual kindness. That could be an unbearable combination. The Mistress is a Witch whose spell is sexual kindness, and as we know from Smart, such Witches are punished, 'just for wearing the lineaments of gratified desire.'[2] A Mistress can overturn, initiate and even conjure new worlds and new lives; sexually, structurally and morally. This is a superpower for which women tend to be burnt, figuratively and literally, at the stake.[3]

In *The Parable of the Sower*, a dystopian novel written by science-fiction pioneer Octavia Butler, the protagonist, Lauren, has a superpower similar to that of the Mistress, that of 'hyper empathy'. This power allows Lauren to not only viscerally share emotions and sensations with others but also generate intergalactic visions of not just life, but of philosophy and morality.[4] This conception of kindness is world-changing and also burgeons throughout Smart's writing about Barker's wife, whom she describes as her 'gentle usurper' and usurped, as killer and killed. Smart also gives this kindness to the world, by relentlessly turning inward and telling her revolutionary story. Her kindness is not reciprocated, yet it has many dimensions, all of them troubling and constantly offering ways to be kind to someone who has been forever an outsider. Smart is exhausted from it, which can be felt through every word of the short text. In the concluding chapter, as the final devastation hits that George has deserted her while she is pregnant with his child, Smart writes: 'By Grand Central Station I sat down and wept: I will *not* be placated by the mechanical motions of existence, nor find consolation in the solicitude of waiters who notice my devastated face.'[5] Smart is raging. While being pulled by the world and its matters and rituals, she is also forced to hide her pain. It is a world that is the wrong shape to receive her story, a world that would prefer she kept quiet, and carried on: 'Well, it's too late to complain, my honey-dove. Yes, it's all over. No regrets. No postmortems.'[6] Let's give Smart the postmortem. Now she, now the Mistress, has our attention; let's look deeper into this sexual kindness that surrounds Mistresses like her. What we will find is a rare superpower that combines sex with kindness, sex with ethics, and the erotic with the revolutionary.

Sex and kindness: rare bedfellows?

We have seen from Smart's story that kindness of any kind is rarely bestowed upon the Mistress. The Mistress might even doubt that she is entitled to kindness, given how she can be treated. In *Signs for Lost Children*, a novel about abusive intimate bonds between mothers and daughters, Sarah Moss reminds us of the sad perception, and often lived truth, particularly for women, that kindness rarely 'finds sexual expression'.[7] Although the Mistress might often testify to this as truth since she is rarely the recipient of kindness – far from it, she is often the victim of abuse and cruelty; she can point incisively to its occurrence, necessity and sexual power. She is often an expert at deploying it. She can show where it is required, and what systems are currently in place to prevent it. But what *is* it? Let me first be clear about the type of kindness that sexual kindness is *not*.

Sexual kindness is not niceness

As Kate Manne reminds us in *Down Girl*, 'kindness is not kindness, if it doesn't come from having the beneficiary's best interests at heart, as one of its motivating factors'.[8] Yet, this must not be in service of a power serving 'good' such as loyalty. In other words, sexual kindness is not manipulation for the benefit of the person pretending to give it. Niceness could also be considered to be the bare minimum, if niceness means treating a person whom you want to have sex with as a human being. But actually, niceness is not kind. It is faux-kindness. Kindness is not lavishing roses, gifts and compliments; it is not manipulation of feeling, and it is not being kind *despite* thinking someone is not worthy of your attention. Sexual kindness is also not requiring a person to have sex with someone because that person says or indicates that they are entitled to it, or acts as though they are entitled to it. Sexual kindness is also not consent. Consent is a legal concept that says both parties must agree to sex. Sexual kindness is much more than basic agreement, which ought to be the bare minimum. Sexual kindness does not excuse racism. Sexual kindness is not an excuse for homophobia, transphobia, biphobia or ableism. Sexual kindness is not using/abusing someone but being polite about it and occasionally chucking in an 'I love you' to make yourself seem kind. Sexual kindness is not seeking out (consciously or not) the vulnerability within a person and using fucking as a simulacrum for giving care. It is not judgement of sexual practices based on your own moral sense of superiority. These acts or ways of using 'kindness' are not sexual kindness at all, but the very opposite: they are *sexual cruelty*. Sexual kindness bursts right through any of these forms of weaponized niceness. Sexual kindness bursts through shackles of propriety and the founding tenets of Western philosophy, morality, society and law, and sees and cares for the whole of the body, how it has suffered and how it can be pleasured.

Sexual kindness is not legal

Joseph Story, one of America's most famous jurists, described the law as a 'jealous mistress'. He went on to say that such a Mistress requires constant courtship and 'is not to be won by trifling favours, but by lavish homage'.[9] Story is both right and wrong. The law is indeed jealous, possessive and requires not only lawyers but everyone to surrender their constant vigilance and respect. But the law is not a Mistress. The law is the opposite of a Mistress, since the law is never kind. Law is the foundation of that very institution that the Mistress threatens, that is so dear to Western morality: marriage. Law is the text that tells the story that adultery is unlawful; that is, in the heteronormative sense that for a man or woman who is married to have penis in vagina sex with another man or woman is a ground for divorce.[10] And so it has been for centuries. The law is not only inside our bodies but between our sheets. Both invited and uninvited presence, the law tells us what we can have and what we cannot, under the guise of protection, in the full knowledge that as humans, we cannot resist forbidden fruit. As French philosopher Michel Foucault argued, by virtue of telling us what desires are 'right', the law pushes us to transgress, or to desire what we cannot, or should not have.[11] Simultaneously, we are taught to renounce temptation and treat it as that which makes us impure along the path to evil.[12] It is not hard to see why revilement of the Mistress as temptress is so engrained within us. She symbolizes both our sexuality and the path towards the punishment that we believe we deserve – and boy, are we angry about it? The law is much more like a jealous husband.

The law, in Smart's story, conceals a multitude of sins. The affair is consensual. And thus, concludes the law's concern for Smart. Remember, consent is underpinned by the idea of agreement, and it is impossible to argue that Smart did not agree to her relationship with Barker. But this does not mean that she is unharmed, nor does it mean that her case does not need investigating.

Yet we see the consistent and persistent devaluation of her sexual being during her affair, and along with it, we are led to witness the law's disdain for the Mistress. Mistresses can be treated very badly. Further, though, Mistresses can be Mistresses against their will. As we know, for the law, Mistresses, like wives, are property. The horror of this idea is shown to spectacular effect in Margaret Atwood's speculative dystopian *The Handmaid's Tale*. Offred is an 'official' (non-consensual) Mistress, whose function, with the (coerced) complicity of the infertile wife, is to have sex with the husband and to produce children, and ultimately to be generally and sexually abused.[13] Atwood's tale might be futuristic and dystopian, but it is also a commentary on the present. The chill can also be felt in the similarity between Atwood's tale and Smart's. Both situations are different, both in time and in space, as well as context, but in both novels we find painful accounts by women controlled (and so inside the law) yet outside of the law's protection. By virtue of her existence, the Mistress undercuts the law, and shows its insider/outsider distinctions to be false.

Enslaved Mistresses

Women have historically been enslaved into being Mistresses, and it is the law that has allowed this to happen. This is the law at its cruellest, most oppressive, and also its most revealing. Mistresses have been made into the property of enslavers and husbands alike. As we know, the law has always allowed husbands to own their wives. For example, English law only abolished the marital rape exception (the law stating that a man cannot rape his wife since she is his property and provides irrevocable consent by virtue of marriage) in 1991.[14] Yet maintaining the idea of women as property is not only to do with sexual access to women's bodies. When women are property, they are also 'under control.' This is not happening in the shadows of a dystopian world but in plain sight. Angela Y. Davis, one of many Black women who taught us how to be radical in reclaiming our bodies, wrote, 'as long as women are viewed as the sexual property of their present or future husbands, their ability to bring about the institutional transformations that will lessen the burden of sexist oppression will be severely limited.'[15]

To understand how the law allows men to own Mistresses as well as wives, it is necessary to draw attention to an important person in American history, Sarah (Sally) Hemings, who is widely acknowledged to have been the enslaved Mistress of Thomas Jefferson.[16] Since racist Jefferson (who believed Black people to be inferior) and his descendants have long denied this relationship, there are little in the way of accounts, particularly from Sally herself. In fact, there are little in the way of stories told by any enslaved Mistresses; rather, available reports focus on the white oppressor and their efforts to silence these stories. Stories generally of Black women's sexuality, independent of colonial narratives, are only starting to become visible in the mainstream. The telling of these stories is fraught with danger for the authors, who face colonial legacies of censorship (by white feminism too) in the form of stereotyping, hyper-sexualization and misogynoir.[17] The incredulity faced by Mistresses is bad enough, but the incredulity towards a woman who is both Black *and* a Mistress? Here we find the hearts of white feminism aflame. The fire is fuelled by colonial entitlement, proprietorship over victimhood and the enforcement of the colonial violence of the gender binary.[18] Colonial power has possessed Mistresses in far more violent ways than it has possessed wives, and the fear of hearing this truth runs deep.

Enslaved Mistresses have had their status as dehumanized and desexualized enshrined by law, which is no surprise since the idea of people as property, the gender binary[19] and 'who could wed and who could bed' are concepts foundational to colonialism.[20] The law determines who can be property, who can be controlled and who can be punished. Enslaved Mistresses, as property, would not have been able to give or refuse consent to sex, since to do so is an attribute of someone who has legal personhood, and not a person who is property, and certainly not a person who is illegitimate property. The protections of being property in the form of being a wife are a respectable (white) woman's privilege, which ensures the domination and subordination of Black women.[21]

Keeping Mistresses

Throughout the enslavement of people, a Black woman would not have been able to consent, since she was denied personhood at law. Post-abolition and into the time of writing, a husband's Mistress would have been able to *technically* refuse to consent, though given the bigoted and sexist attitudes of judges and juries, it is unlikely that any case of sexual assault or rape brought by her would be sympathetically received. Her personhood would be more insidiously denied, through rape myths, and a belief that a Mistress is always free to do what she wants, and therefore to consent. The husband might 'take' a wife from her personhood, but he might also 'keep' a Mistress from her personhood.[22]

The idea of a Mistress as an illegitimate form of property is also present in eighteenth-century literature. Novels such as the eighteenth-century epistolary *Pamela; or Virtue Rewarded* by Samuel Richardson tie a woman's morality and worth to her ability to remain, or become, the official property of men.[23] If we then zip forward in time, to the bleak futures of Atwood's *The Handmaid's Tale*, we find a perfect reflection of this and the idea of Mistresses as legal and moral property. Offred's body is seen as property; even her name denotes this status; she is 'of' her master ('*Of-Fred*') and her validity and existence is inextricably tied to her fidelity to her Master. Her entire body, including her sexuality, is reduced to property, so it can be controlled and regulated. She is to have sex with the husband, willingly or not, and she is to bear (but not keep) his children. She is not entitled to rights, since she is property. She can be punished at any time and lives in a state of constant vigilance.

I do not argue that all Mistress relationships are non-consensual, far from it. But I do argue that legal structures, which uphold colonial and toxic philosophies of gender, monogamy and women's sexuality, bring us, as a society, to treat Mistresses badly, and less than human. The Mistress's sexual kindness is forever in defiance of this, and this is what makes her virtue both surprising and powerful. She is a huge threat to the law because she is intimately close to it. The law is an abusive married lover, a tyrannical lawmaker. He is a cross between 'The Demand Man' and 'Mr Right' from the list of types of abusive partner described in Lundy Bancroft's revelatory and essential text on abusive men and relationships, *Why Does He Do That? Inside the Minds of Angry and Controlling Men*.[24] The law wants there to be Mistresses, and needs them so it can 'keep' them, but there is no room for her to have a desire of her own. The law is at the root of our compulsion to claim and keep Mistresses as property, yet deny their presence and keep them in secret. And as Angela Y. Davis told us, we must urgently grasp at that root,[25] and overthrow the law, and ourselves, if necessary.

Sexual kindness is (sort of) ethical

The Mistress flouts the law by being in opposition to it, while also being used and abused by it. She is glorious and brave, while also being tragic. She is Marilyn Monroe, Moll Flanders and she is Shae in *Game of Thrones* defying the Lannisters, consistently strong and defiant, but ultimately strangled by her lover.[26] She is a constant threat since at any moment she might 'out' us all, while also outing the whole of Western law and society. She is Julie Gayet (former Mistress to Francois Hollande); she has a power, if she were allowed (and able) to speak out. We are starting to see that the Mistress's unique position as outside of law and therefore outside of protection and what Western society has named 'right' and 'good' means rightness and goodness is never on her side. As we have seen, her lack of protection ranges from having no rights within her relationship, as a wife would have, to not being legally able to consent, in the most extreme circumstances. Since the Mistress's position in society is so changeable, often because it is not desirable to society to allow her personhood, she cannot avail herself of conventional sexual ethics. She cannot appeal to 'right' and 'wrong' rules of living, because she is, by default, always 'wrong', and therefore no 'wrong' can be done to her, since she is the one, literally, in the 'wrong'. The Mistress relies on something else in relationships, something closer to sexual kindness: sexual ethics, but not as we know them.

An ethic of her own?

Mistress ethics are ethics written by, and for, the Mistress. So where should we look and where should the Mistresses look in order to understand these ethics? For sure, not to philosophers of ethics, for reasons I shall explore in the next chapter. The answer is inward, to herself, and others like her. Her ethics must be unlike any other, since she is facing something unique. In every act, through every moment in her sexual life, she receives the full force of judgement. This happens every time she says, 'I am a Mistress', every time the world comes to know she is a Mistress, but also every day in her relationships with her lovers, and those with whom she shares these relationships. What we will see is that she needs an ethical foundation that allows her to set her own rules. Consequently, the first step along the journey to *Mistress Ethics* is in deciding that, as a Mistress, you are entitled to a form ethics; more than that, you are entitled to kindness as a bare minimum.

The Mistress has slutty ethics! Untrue!

Let's first consider where some of the obvious places might be that she might start to look for answers. She might naturally begin with the ever-revolutionary *The Ethical Slut*.[27] In some ways, the ethics of the Mistress will share some of the characteristics of the ethics of the Slut, but for a few crucial differences which flow from the fundamental differences between identifying as a Slut, or as a Mistress. Let's begin with the similarities: the Mistress is absolutely into the idea at the core of *The Ethical Slut*, that sex is nice and pleasure is good for you. She holds it close to her heart, and many other parts of her body, if it feels good. It is also likely to be the case that she believes sexuality *should* be celebrated, no matter your gender. Like the Slut, the Mistress also has a problem with the link automatically drawn between morality and a woman's sexuality experience, whom she sleeps with and how.[28]

It is important to understand though that the Mistress exists, and importantly, fucks, in exact opposition to what society has proclaimed right-fucking. She knows her sexuality 'should' be celebrated, but she also knows that it *won't* be. This is because of her position as outside of the marriage, outside of convention and what is acceptable bedroom activity. She knows she simply won't be celebrated, no matter how much she believes she 'should' be. In fact, by virtue of her explicit opposition, she is punished by society, but perhaps also (directly or indirectly) by her lover. The Mistress also understands the move to reclaim the word 'Slut' is crucial, but for her it is complicated. To be able to do so can be a privilege. The Mistress may not wish to identify as a 'Slut' at all, but more so, if she did, this could place her in danger, since she could be 'outing' herself as a Mistress (or indeed she might be outing her sexual orientation, depending on the genders of those in the relationship). It could be dangerous for her to shamelessly reclaim 'Slut' for even reclaiming any sexuality might be dangerous for her. Letting her be a Slut if she likes is not going to help her attack what caused the need for reclamation in the first place. Black women have also been branded immoral Mistresses, through stereotypes such as 'jezebel', which has been used to justify all manner of atrocities. Reclaiming 'Slut' for Black women is not enough, since Black women forced to require solidarity and the acceptance of a racist society, before being safe (in all respects) to claim their inner Slut. It is just not so simple.[29] It is also often the case that a community of Sluts is unwilling to accept the Mistress as one of their own, since her 'morality' is too loose, even for them. As Wednesday Martin writes in the revolutionary *Untrue*, which debunks many treasured myths about women's sexuality and fidelity, 'among progressives, especially those who describe themselves as "sex positive," female sexual self-determination may be tolerated, even lauded. But in their world, a woman who has an *affair* is still likely to be considered or called something much worse than "self-determined" for having done so.'[30]

The Ethical Slut shows us the battlefield, but the Mistress is, through and through, a warrior, seeking a law of her own. As such, she needs more help than being given permission to reclaim something that she never asked for. To the world, she is an 'adulteress' – she lusts and she cheats; she is fighting against a world aflame and affronted.[31] As Martin writes, the woman who rejects monogamy is brave, and such women are desperate, dying even, for this harmful foundation of our normality to be redefined.[32] The Mistress is thus forced to be braver beyond the Slut. She is fighting judgements, every day, throughout history and she will be, into hopefully only imagined, dystopian futures. She deserves her own ethics.

Oh Yes! Sexual kindness is orgasmic!

The Mistress is orgasmic. I mean exactly this: her whole being and identity, and therefore her ethics, are orgasmic. Let me explain. I do not mean that she walks around with a perpetually wet vagina and swollen vulva (if these were even indeed reliable indicators for arousal). Nor do I mean that she is in a constant state of afterglow, having reached a dramatic climax; nor is she constantly fucking, nor ready for fucking. Instead, it is her refusal for her sexuality to be limited by the constraints of relationship structures which brings her in touch with the revolutionary and kind power of the erotic. In short, it is her sexual kindness that makes her orgasmic.

Mistresses are often also philosophers – Anaïs Nin, for example. Thinking deeply and writing about her experiences as Nin did was a survival strategy, and lead to the formation of a canon for other Mistresses to read and in which to take solace and inspiration. Before consulting the wisdom of aspects of Nin's work, let us consider the power of flesh and fluid orgasmic sex to overturn the way we think. As a Mistress I was drawn to Nin's philosophies, and all kinds of philosophies that found a power in sex that is so great, that it can disorientate everything we think we know about it.

French philosopher Gilles Deleuze and his writing partner, anarchic psychoanalyist Felix Guattari, imagined a particularly powerful concept, called the Body without Organs.[33] Sexy as hell, it allows you to take on any sexual identity (and sex) that you can imagine. It lets you bust through your identity along the waves of your desire and become one with sex itself, 'an open zone of possibility: desiring-machines or the nonhuman sex: not one or even two sexes, but *n* sexes'.[34] You can be whoever you want in the bedroom, and do such things as sing with your vulva, grow a penis and become a field of anuses. The concept captures the imagination, but also the body. Deleuze and Guattari find the orgasm 'deplorable', since the (male orgasm) has determined what is deemed by society as acceptable sexual orientation, and acceptable heteronormative sex.[35] Deleuze and Guattari are indeed justified in proclaiming this kind of orgasm deplorable, since we find exactly the mechanisms by which she (and indeed us all) is harmed – our sexual hierarchies atop of which sits heterosexual monogamy. What if we reclaim the idea for the Mistress, and turn it on its head. What if, instead, we followed the orgasm (or indeed non-orgasm, and every kind of orgasm as Annamarie Jagose's *Orgasmology* tells us we must)[36] of women, in particular, Mistresses? What *kind* of sexuality might we find?

Finding kind sexuality?

As we trace the orgasm (or indeed, non-orgasm) line within a *kind sexuality*, we should find a woman who grows in strength within her sexual encounters. When we do this for the Mistress, however, this is rarely what we will find. This is because of the weight of the law, her identity and the resoluteness with which we have been taught, and are still taught, that extra-marital sex is wrong and therefore *she* is wrong. It is as though without the protection of rightness in our society, the Mistress is not entitled to sexual kindness, nor would she be capable of giving it. The idea that a body should be enhanced and strengthened through relationships should not be a revolutionary one, but when it comes to Mistresses, it is. As well as giving us the horny 'Body without Organs', Gilles Deleuze gives us a form of ethics which is rooted in the body, rather than conventional philosophical morality. Developing the philosophy of Baruch Spinoza, Deleuze gives us the idea that what is ethical or 'right' in a situation makes the body stronger, and what is not, makes it weaker.[37] What makes the body stronger or weaker will depend on that particular body, and also, crucially, the way it is marginalized by conventional and dominant thinking. Suddenly, life is filled with ethical moments, and no more so than with the Mistress, whose close contact with the erotic, with sex, with relationships and their regulation keeps her in a constant state of revolution, danger and possibility. It should not be a surprise, however, that it is difficult to think of the Mistress as deserving of being subject to even these terms, especially since, as the philosopher Julia Kristeva reminds us, Spinoza explicitly excluded women (along with 'children and lunatics') from ethics.[38]

Sexual kindness requires not only a stronger body for the Mistress but also good sex. While I was a Mistress I read philosophy, but I also read erotica. I learnt much more from the latter. I saw that powerful desire was also kind. This was far from what I had been led to believe. It is not hard to find erotica written by Mistresses – it is their philosophy. Anaïs Nin, one of the most famous Mistresses, and an extraordinary writer and philosopher of sex, was Mistress to (among others) Henry Miller. *Spy in the House of Love* is a story about a Mistress, or someone who might *have* a Mistress. Her protagonist Sabina is a 'spy in the international house of love'.

Sabina is a warrior and explorer, seeking the best sex she can find, 'At night too, she puzzled the mystery of her desperate need of kindness. As other girls prayed for handsomeness in a lover, or for wealth, or for power, or for poetry, she had prayed fervently: let him be kind.'[39] At the time, I thought it strange that of all the ways I was now learning that it was possible to express desire, that a desire for kindness would be the expression of desire that Nin would have Sabina prize the most. I was also surprised at how aroused I became when I read the telephone conversation that compiles Nicholson Baker's *Vox*[40] (famously gifted to Bill Clinton by his then Mistress, Monica Lewinsky). There is a generosity within this desire, a feeling of safety between the two pervert lovers despite the impermanence of the encounter, which allows their desires to take flight in ways that I had never read about before. It is a conversation the likes of which I had wished for with my married lover at the time when I asked if he still had sex with his wife. I express a fantasy for this kind conversation at the end of my own story with a married lover in *Fucking Law*.[41] The conversation sadly remained a fantasy, until I was a Mistress again, with a different person.

Sexual kindness is revolutionary

Kindness in sex is something that we are not used to encountering, much less seeing as something that the Mistress might elicit, or be deserving of. I argue that this is partially attributable to what Alison Phipps has called in *Me Too, Not You*, 'the outrage economy', which has rendered us hungry for agitation, thriving off of sexuality scandal, particularly relating to women.[42] Such scandals (which often involve proprietorship over white women's victimhood, such as #MeToo, despite #MeToo being a movement generated by Tarana Burke, a Black activist) usually include a commensurate demand for punishment by a third party (usually the police or the courts, which are known to be misogynist and racist institutions).[43] Mistresses have also caused agitation and outrage, not by cynical design like Jordan Peterson or trans-exclusionary feminists such as JK Rowling, nor by being a permitted (white) 'victim' of #MeToo. Rather, they cause, and have always caused, outrage by virtue of being women who have sex outside of what is 'acceptable' women's desire for straight, monogamous, married motherhood, but also by showing that, actually, this sex, and this way of being, could be revolutionary. She scares powerful people. Mistresses have been punished for centuries, in every moment of their everyday lives, as well as being literally burnt at the stake.[44] Think of the stories we know (some of which I will tell in the next chapter) and the stories there are that we have not heard and that are kept secret at all costs (often at the cost of the Mistress's own story, her dignity, her joys, her pleasure and her full unapologetic personhood).

Audre Lorde has been telling us for a long time about the power of the erotic (not the pornographic, which for her, is the opposite) as both profoundly creative and profoundly feared, by those in power in this racist, patriarchal and anti-erotic society.[45] To be in touch with it is to walk the 'bridge' that connects the spiritual with the political, and to be persistently battling states 'supplied' to us, such as self-denial, self-effacement and resignation.[46] The erotic is also disorientating, since it demands that 'satisfaction is possible and does not have to be called *marriage* nor *god*.[47] The Mistress is compelled to be in touch with the erotic, since the sex she has is always wrong, constantly judged – so too is her body, for being outside of what is ethical in the conventional sense. The need for kindness, as well as its revolutionary power, expands exponentially in line with the frequency that a given body is in touch with the erotic.

The erotic is not simply a sexual power but a general connective force, compelling us to do what is kind, but not necessarily what is easy. Unlike niceness, there is room within kindness to respond with fury, rage and passion. It can demand change and responses that are not easy. Kindness is, at its heart, a love ethic, which as bell hooks wrote in *all about love*, living such an ethic is fundamentally active and means to let that love guide, and become, behaviour.[48] You can't fake it and you can't signal it. Kindness is fucking hard work. For Lorde, in our duty to the erotic, and part of this love ethic, we must not 'turn away' from our experience. To turn away is to abuse those who participate within our experiences.[49] To turn inward, meaning to see fully the virtues of kindness in a given situation, or to make a body stronger rather than weaker, is what is required by the erotic, and what is often required of the Mistress. My duty to her, as writer of this book, and you as reader, is to do her some kindness, to hooks-love her, and not to turn away. To turn away from her is to abuse someone whose experience of the erotic shows us what is wrong with our relationship structures. Instead we must turn towards her, while we turn to ourselves, and see how she experiences the erotic, and how she is made stronger and weaker in ways we did not expect. When we use *this* method to trace the orgasmic line while hearing her story, we can begin to carve out a way of being kind that is tailored to the Mistress.

This will be sexual kindness. So, our first task in understanding and learning sexual kindness is to commit to seeing and listening to the Mistress. And what might we hear? Some might suggest there won't be much, since the stories have all been told in books, films and salacious news stories. This is wrong. It is sad too, since there is a deep mine of magic to be found in some surprising places. I know for sure that there are a million stories concealed within identikit cheap hotel rooms.

This first set of bullet points is a taster. There is much more and it will all start to come out; now it has started. Every Mistress is infinitely different, and each will have radically different experiences. Yet, there will be something common to them all: sexual kindness or the possibility for it. Read this list, and as you do, see where kindness is hiding, waiting to be given. Because of her perceived lack of virtue, it is hard to see her, so the shape of her desire, and her fight, eludes us. Because of this, so does its superpower. This is no accident, for our attention must be maintained on what is virtuous, productive and 'good'; lest we slip, let things slip or let ourselves to become slippery, or reveal the slippery revolutionary, the Mistress, who is within us all. Let's take this forbidden journey, enter that scary space and find out who she is, and who we are.

- Turning towards her, we see her alone in her hotel room, sitting upon white bed linen. *Stranger than Kindness* plays.[50] We see her sat in the hotel restaurant. The manufactured light shines on her at just around dinner time. She eats a sad steak and drinks a bad wine, alone. Her lover has had to go home for dinner with his family.

- We see her puzzled eyes and the dip of her head when a new acquaintance asks if she is married or in a relationship. When she answers, 'Yes,' we see her anticipation of the follow-up questions, during which her Mistress status will be outed. They might be kind, but they probably won't be. The acquaintance will project their insecurities upon her. She'll likely be demonized, possibly shunned from friendships and social groups. It feels awkward, perhaps dangerous to be around her. Perhaps it's contagious.

- She fucks her lover and has mind-blowing orgasms. She feels guilt and shame. She's not allowed this pleasure, since it's wrong. She doesn't want to feel shame. She's a Slut and she's proud, as she's been told to be. But she's not ethical, at least she doesn't think so, based on the conversations she's heard and had, and what her mother and grandma taught her. The films, TV, books and the feeling she gets in public, when she sees people interact, tell her she should feel shame. So she feels it, all the time.

- She's alone at home, in a small flat. She has had a horrific day, and her lover has not been able to even call her, since he's at home with his wife and not at work. She wants to be held, more than anything. Her skin hungers.

- She falls ill. It's just a bad cold, but she's exhausted and it knocks her off her feet. She lives alone. She thinks of his wife, who has those warm arms. She wants them, and that soup she makes, but she wants it to be made *just* for her. Her body longs to be healed.

- It's Christmas time and her mother phones her to tell her that her sister is bringing her new boyfriend home to meet the family. Mistress has a boyfriend too, a partner actually, but she cannot bring him home, since he has another home to be in. While she sits uncoupled at her family's dinner table, he'll be sat with his wife. The Christmas crackers, presents, joy and cosy fires will all be the same or similar. They'll feel different for each person in each household. But even more different for her. She wonders if she's capable of feeling like her mother or sister, who seem to have it all figured out. There *must* be something wrong with her.

- She holds a secret. Every moment of everyday. She walks along the high street. Does the woman behind her in the post office queue know? She looked at her in an odd way. Judgement, it looked like, written across her face, as the thoughts rush through her mind: You're that woman they talk about. The wild one. *Homewrecker*. Needs help. Mother should have taught her better.

- She waits. She was once told by a man that 'love waits'. Women wait, usually for men, if they love them. But she really does wait; she has learnt to. She waits for judgement from men, from every person and every space and situation designed for a relationship that is not the one she is having, a sexuality that is not hers. She waits for punishment. It usually comes. She has been told different, especially in these modern times, by modern thinkers, modern sex, but nonetheless she suspects she deserves it. And she gets it.

- When her married lover hurts her and abuses her, she knows everyone is thinking she deserves it. In fact, she should have expected it! She is trespassing on property that is not hers. How daft she is. Two of them raped her. Two of them hit her. All of them abused her, one way or another. She always deserved it. She's a bitch, a whore, a slut, bad woman, fallen, witch, whatever – she asked for it.

- Friends judge her. They don't want to meet her lover and find his presence disgusting, and therefore her, too. This makes her angry, since he is one of the kind ones. She lost one friend, who thought that she would steal her boyfriend because that is just 'what she does'.

- It's a witch hunt once it all comes out (it always does). It's a cruel ousting. Gossip at the back of the bus, turning up at her work. It's blame for her, forgiveness for him, poor fallible man, but men will be men. Pitchforks at dawn.

- It's the work Summer Party. Partners welcome (not hers, and not her).

- He's not faithful to her. Does she need to be faithful to him? Does he want her to be? Does she hope he wants her to be? What does faithful mean, anyway? Why is it so important to everyone? Come to think of it, what does faith have to do with sex, anyway?

- She has rarely seen her story told. She does not know what to expect, other than punishment. She's given up trying to tell hers since it results in being told to be quiet (people don't want to hear that sort of thing).

- You are wrong. You're always inherently wrong, because you're a Mistress, and Mistresses are wrong.

- She's not a bad person. She looks in the mirror and tells herself a thousand times a day. She doesn't believe it.

- Her lover is not wrong, though; it is expected. But he's with another, not only in bed but in every moment, every interaction. His rightness is reflected in culture, society and law. How could she be a match for all this?

- She wants to talk to her lover. Should she call? Better not. Even a text could be risky these days, with the notifications showing on the lock screen. Perhaps an email, but then computers sync with phones these days; what if she's using his laptop? Better write a letter. It's like screaming into the void.

- No one will be on her side, no matter what happens. She, the wife, was there first. This is what counts. They won't see what happened, who did what, or the minutiae of pain. They'll see it in black and white, right and wrong. She'll be asked to explain, though, but the explanation will not be enough. She'll be pitied. She didn't ask for it.

- There will be a question, when she's walking with her lover, such as 'How do you two know each other?' The answer cannot be she's my girlfriend.

- Your lover may also never see you for who you are, since he, too, has been taught since the beginning that you are wrong and that you do not matter. It's not his fault.

- She lacks kindness, for she lacks virtue.

Story Part II: Who do you think you are?

My beloved concubine, my Sugar from *The Crimson Petal and the White*, you are. You are a 'Miss', not the type to be a 'Mrs'. You are Elizabeth Smart. You are Alicia Keys, and your 'victim' is Mashonda. You are Amber Heard, beginning your relationship with Johnny Depp as his Mistress having met him on the set of *The Rum Diary*,[51] but now, you have been named his abuser (lucky the court didn't buy this story, this time).[52] The danger is that if you start as a Mistress, you will always be a deceiver. Your 'victim' is Vanessa Paradis. You are definitely Angelina Jolie, a witch, drinking her lover's blood, while Jennifer Anniston is the perfect wife, dignified and adored. You are Mia Isabella, you are a trans woman, and Mistress to the rapper Tyga. You are a French royal Mistress Jeanne-Antoinette de Pompadour, Mistress to King Louis XV, or Françoise-Athénaïs de Rochechouart, Mistress to King Louis XIV. You are Harriet Jacobs. You are Hannah Arendt. You are Victoria Brooks. You are Vita Sackville-West, or are you *Orlando*? You are Simone de Beauvoir. Name a philosopher, you will find a Mistress. You are Marilyn Monroe. You are Jane Eyre, or you are Anna Karenina. You are Vera, tortured into being Lavrenti Pavlovich Beria's accomplice.[53] You are in *Game of Thrones* as Shae or Ellaria Sand. You are Sofie Vissa and your victim is Jennifer Lopez. Gentleman Jack. You are Anne Lister, writing the stories of your secret love affairs with women in a secret code, where you kindly mark your orgasms (for us to trace) with an 'x'. You are Mistress to the law, which finds your desire for women publishable. You are also a Mistress of your married lover, Mariana. She is ashamed to be seen in public with you; meanwhile you are broken by the thought of Mariana in bed with her husband. You are Bess, with your sexual kindness to the Duchess of Devonshire bold, arousing and full of rage. You are the many Mistresses of Castro, or Boris Johnson, or name another powerful politician, find a Mistress. You are Monica Lewinsky. You are Camilla Parker-Bowles, or Princess Margaret. You are Catherine Walston, Mistress of Graham Greene, written into the *End of the Affair*. Your dedication in the book reads only as 'C'. One letter of a whole story. You are Wanda in *Venus in Furs*; you are Irma in *The Balcony*, tirelessly playing out fantasies for those ignorant to the revolution, while you *are* it. Sometimes you are a sex worker – sometimes officially, sometimes paid, sometimes not. If not, you might feel a camaraderie with sex workers that you cannot quite put into words. You are pathologized. You are you; you are me; you are us. Myth and fantasy, as well as fear, form our perception of you. You are so many people, so many things, but really, who is she? Who are you?

2

Whore! Wife! Pervert! Mother! Who is a Mistress and who has a Mistress?

This shit just got personal

If you have made it this far, then you will know that I write not just *about* Mistresses but *as* a Mistress. Lisa Taddeo's intimate novel, *Three Women,* is based on stories she has been told, as a researcher, by real women about their lives. She writes that there are reasons when and why women's stories are believed.[1] When we are talking about women's stories, they are not simply believed, by virtue of being told, but are distorted by the political and legal lens through which people hear and read them. There is always an argument to be made about a woman's life. Yet, when Taddeo tells these stories, she asks us, as readers, to witness them alongside her. You witness things you do not think that you should, like when we are asked to witness Sloane witness her husband fucking another woman in front of her, for the first time. We witness her witness the curve of his back with each thrust. It is painful, but we must see it. This is because the author knows that a witness is an essential part of a story. And you are now bearing witness to the Mistress's story, and I know that this story will be hard to hear without passing judgement since it is a woman's story, and it is about sex.

When it comes to Mistresses, the default position is assumption, myth and fear. It is also assumed that the Mistress lies. This is shown dramatically in the BBC television drama *The Cry*, a story of a Mistress, Joanna, who becomes a wife, and whose husband murders their baby, yet manipulates Joanna not only into thinking she did it (when, spoiler-alert: he did it) but into orchestrating a cover-up of their baby's death, which involves a nationwide search. Joanna eventually confronts her husband, and ultimately murders him. In one of the courtroom scenes, the prosecution barrister asks her how 'we' are meant to believe her in relation to anything, given that she is an 'adulteress'.[2] Being a Mistress means that not only is it hard for your story to be told but it will not be believed if it is. It is necessary for witnesses to understand how important it is to listen and believe Mistresses about their stories; otherwise, we miss opportunities for sexual kindness.

The author of *The Mistress: History, Myths and Interpretations of the 'Other Woman'*, Victoria Griffin, herself a Mistress, was criticized since she (as she absolutely must) blurs the lines between fact and fiction, personal and impersonal, analysis and myth, history and present.[3] The criticism is not a surprise, given how she uses her personal authority to demand attention to some unpleasant truths about ourselves. This is because the author has drawn us into her world, and now we cannot deny what we see. It is also a weird space, where law and rules cease to exist, or cease to have an impact. Law and rules have nothing to do with what we feel, or what is right, right? And this scares us. This is a space where things get weird and serious. As Arabella (played by Michaela Coel), in a therapy session for sexual assault survivors in the BBC television series *I May Destroy You*,[4] puts it – we can get a *really close* look at what is going on in this in-between storytelling space, without rules to tell us what to think and what to do – we have the story, and nothing else. Elizabeth Abbott's epic *Mistresses: A History of the Other Woman* is an intricate and important account that exposes all manner of historical Mistresses and Mistress-keepers. While she skilfully exposes these stories, we must look harder, and deeper; beyond the idea that Mistresses are living out their 'fantasies' of being with powerful destructive men, in order to understand what causes men to abuse their Mistresses, or otherwise, 'have', rather than 'hold', them in sexual kindness. So, let's get personal.

Marie Curie, the Witch

Marie Curie is a typical Mistress. In the film *Radioactive*, the soon-to-be Mrs Marie Curie says to her prospective husband, Pierre, as they stand together at the start of the film, in electric flirtation: 'I will not be your Mistress',[5] and so becomes his wife. After the untimely death of her husband, she does indeed become a Mistress, to someone else's husband. Despite her huge part in revolutionizing cancer treatment by developing a theory of radioactivity, which also led to the development of mobile X-ray technology, her extraordinary strength, intellect and super-human kindness, it is at this point that she is rejected by society. Her Mistress status comes before all that she has done for science, before her Nobel Prizes in physics and chemistry, rendering her an outcast. It is her challenge to marriage that becomes more important than her science, and even her ability to save lives. There will be those that see the film, and despite her revolutionary status in history, will still see her period as a Mistress as a 'stain' upon her record.

From watching the film, it is her status as a Mistress that causes Curie to be rejected by society, but also xenophobic and nationalist discrimination by virtue of her being Polish. Marie Curie is treated as an outsider and outcast. This is also an example of a Mistress who has bestowed a great general kindness but who has not received sexual kindness in return. It is as though her sexuality is not entitled to kindness, though the rest of her might be. This means that in reality none of her receives it, since kindness, as we know from Chapter 1, sees and receives the whole of someone. Marie Curie is an outsider, by virtue of her nationality, but also her sexuality. In *Witches, Sluts, Feminists*, Kristen Sollée convincingly aligns rebellion and revolution, as well as sexual independence, with witchcraft. Marie Curie is a typical Mistress, and typical Witch. Sollée makes me rejoice in being a Witch, and indeed a Mistress, since it is all the things I had dreamed of being – a sexual sorceress and fornicator, feminist revolutionary and bitch through and through. Yet strangely, the rest of the world does not seem to see it this way.[6] Witch-hood, like Mistress-hood, is something that is at once revolutionary and punishable by death. We wanted Marie Curie's science, and her safe revolution, but we did not want her revolutionary sex: we did not want her as a Mistress. As Virginia Woolf noted in *A Room of One's Own*, when we read about the history of witches, there is likely an obscured tale of a 'lost novelist' or 'suppressed poet',[7] or in short, a revolutionary and creative woman, likely a writer, who terrified the world with her powers.

Like the Witch, the Mistress cannot win. Sexuality and revolution are a combination that will get you killed, not just by the baying crowd but sometimes too by the husband you are fucking. As a combination of both Art Witch and a Political Witch,[8] as well as pain-in-the-cunt argumentative Witch, I have received exactly this kick in the teeth. On the face of it, a Mistress such as I could be seen as the fantasy that combines intelligence and sexuality. I was a graduate student researching sexuality. And so, I would inevitably fall from my lofty perch quickly and indeed I did fall. I went from an exciting object of curiosity and obsession to (upon articulation of my needs) being deceptive, manipulative and adaptive because I became a threat rather than a fantasy. And at the time, I was naive and I was bamboozled. I thought I was everything a man might want in a Mistress. Of course, I was right, but to the same extent I was wrong. Again, he wanted the sex, but only if it was controlled, and owned by him. He did not want my Witch, and therefore, really, did not want my Mistress.

As much as I was his Mistress, I was also, de facto, a Witch. I had to be, since in his eyes, I was insatiable. He would often talk of me getting 'wet' at the thought or touch of certain men (that he perceived as threats), or in situations when he thought that I ought to, given his fantasy of me. These fantasies resisted even my protestations to the contrary; such was his belief in my witchery. Sollée reminds us that this is a centuries-old belief which dates back to 1486, and I'm sure further back: 'all witchcraft comes from carnal lust, which is, in women, insatiable.'[9] There was nothing I could do, no matter the sexual kindness I extended to him in the form of patience, rage and absorption of this abuse that would ever render him able to reciprocate. To him, the only option was punishment.

Whether Marie Curie or Angelina Jolie, you cannot win. You can be the most virtuous of scientists or the most virtuoso of actresses; you can be a million things, but as a Mistress you will always be a Witch, and for this you will always be punished. The Mistress is indeed insatiable and multi-dextrous. Her desire blushes with witchy over-throwing warmth construed as 'sin'. It is not her generosity, her orgasmic possibility, her playfulness, her rage-filled revolution, nor otherwise her sexual kindness that is seen as insatiable, but her sin. It is helpful to think about the Mistress as a Witch, since we can see how much of a disturbance the combination of sexuality and resistance can be. Perhaps then there is something to learn here – perhaps the Mistress's witchcraft is something to be admired, not punished?

My sexual kindness is as sweet as Sugar's

Our disdain for Mistresses can be matched by our disdain for sex workers. As a Mistress several times in my life, I have often been called a 'whore' or 'prostitute'. If I were following modern sex-positive takes, I would have reclaimed these words and shoved them right back, saying, 'Yes, I am a slut, and so fucking what? You might be repressing your sexuality but here I am – a brave warrior! Suck my strap-on.' But this call to reclamation came too late for me. These messages did not enter my working-class environment, through my education, at a time when I needed them. Inevitably, these words instead landed as insults and trauma cement, meaning that later, when married lovers would hand me cash for half of the hotel bill (since they could not pay on their credit cards, for fear of their wives observing a suspicious transaction), I heard them again. I had internalized a fear of sex workers, and of being a sex worker, all the while feeling a certain camaraderie.

In the television adaptation of Michel Faber's *The Crimson Petal and the White*,[10] Sugar (played by Romola Garai) is a working-class flame-haired sex worker, with lips as feathers, who catches the eye of feckless writer and aristocrat, William Rackham, in a dingy brothel in Victorian London. Sugar is writing a novel of her own, and while she is doing so, the married William Rackham pays her to remain exclusively his property. Agnes (played by Amanda Hale), William's wife, who is always dressed in white, is apparently 'mad' and refuses to acknowledge the existence of their daughter, Sophie. William eventually moves Sugar into the marital home, employing her as Sophie's governess. As time moves on, Agnes becomes increasingly unstable and comes to believe Sugar is her guardian angel sent to heal her. I shall avoid spoiling the rest of the story for those who have not seen the series, nor read Faber's novel, but suffice to say it does not end well for William.

Sweet Sugar rages

The most interesting relationship here is between the two women, Sugar and Agnes. Agnes sees a healing power in Sugar's presence that borders on a romantic desire. She also feels camaraderie with Sugar, since it is revealed that Agnes is clearly being abused by her doctors. There is a moving unity between the two women that makes William appear all the more feckless. Sugar's sexual kindness here takes the form of an extreme resilience, and also through the transcendent connections between women – whether between Sugar and Agnes, or between Sugar and Sophie, with whom she ultimately runs away. The two women also ardently fight the stereotypes imposed upon them. There is the wife's milky innocence (an image that also crops up in *By Grand Central Station*)[11] but also of Sugar the sex worker who is both healer and hater, health-giver and threat. The possibility of her healing William through her sexual kindness, healing his loneliness and healing his literary failure, is always imminent, alongside her gory fantasies of slitting his throat.

Sugar's sexual kindness is the kind that has room for rage, and the recognition of trauma, and the possibility of healing through the connection between women. The camaraderie between wife and her husband's sex worker is hard to access, yet this is where the diamond is found. This is the power of Audre Lorde's erotic. Ask yourself, where does that camaraderie take you? What does it do to you when you turn inward? Sugar tells us, just look for that diamond – look for where sexual kindness is not expected to be returned, and that is where you might find it, and when you might give and/or receive it. Unfortunately, this erotic camaraderie (in the Audre Lorde sense of connecting through profound sexual power)[12] is not felt universally among feminists. Trans exclusion and sex-worker exclusion seem to come hand in hand, along with exclusion of Black women and women of colour.[13] White feminism is not a home for Mistress Ethics. And Mistress Ethics must be hand in hand with sex-worker ethics, since between them, there is the camaraderie of kindness. Sex workers have often been described or depicted as health workers (while having their own rights, health and safety needs persistently ignored, particularly trans sex workers).[14] Sex work is sexual kindness. Sex work carries that hallmark of not being returned, since it cannot be so, within a system that abuses. Sex work, and sexual kindness, like the health work of nurses, is sophisticated kindness work.[15] As Christie Watson points out in *A Language of Kindness*, the truth of nursing, and the practice of kindness, is philosophy, psychology, art, ethics and politics, and also that we have all nursed at some point in our lives.[16] As much as the nurse ought to be lauded for her sophisticated practice, so ought the sex worker, so ought the Mistress, with her special skills. Such an appreciation of her ought to mean that we find ways to reciprocate kind with kind. Understanding how we can be kind to sex workers helps us understand how we can be kind to Mistresses. Sexual kindness is always unexpected.

She is the perfect mother

I grew up believing that I could not be both maternal and sexual, and by logical extension, both Mistress and mother. This was a belief reinforced for me by various husbands (not mine), and one in particular, who told me there was something profoundly erotic about the maternal, which his wife possessed and I did not. That I confessed to wanting a child with him was, he was convinced, due to my will to manipulate him into believing that I was worth leaving his wife. I am curious about the origin of the apparent incompatibility of the figures of Mistress and mother. Do you see a Mistress, in life, or in TV/Film, and automatically think of her as a mother, or wanting to be a mother? It is curious, isn't it, that first we perceive the Mistress as being overtly sexual, or seeing her as sexual before anything else, and also, as not being motherly. Logically, if we see the Mistress as sexual, and of course she will be assumed to be heterosexual, and we see 'straight' sex as fulfilling a reproductive function, then surely the Mistress ought to be a natural mother.

Philosopher Julia Kristeva explores this reticence in us to afford the 'other', in this case women who give birth, the same logic and ethics as everyone else, in her experimental reflection on the birth of her son, *Stabat Mater* (a hymn to the suffering of the Virgin Mary at the Crucifixion, as per the Western Christian tradition).[17] She argues that women tend not to be thought of as subject to ethics as we conventionally, morally, understand them to be, since ethics are built for men by philosophers like Spinoza. This is why we struggle to think of women (and I claim Mistresses, in particular) as entitled to ethical treatment. There is also an important feminist point to consider – if women do not want to be like the men that oppress them, then why would they want to be subject by the same (fucked) moral standards? If women are to have their own ethics, we must divorce conventional morality. Excitingly, it is through the realignment of our ideas of mistress-hood and motherhood that this ethical divorce can take place. For Kristeva, these 'divorced ethics' are called 'Herethics' – heretical and hers, and literally born of the flesh divided.[18] The birthing body points to *the most fundamental* question that haunts humanity and philosophy: can we ever be joined to another? What does it mean to be 'other' than, just yourself? Motherhood knows what it is to be more than one person, and to have another person's life and fate tied intimately to your own. Herethics bridges the divide that conventional ethics makes between people, and asks us instead to think of our fates, our actions, desires and experiences, as conjoined. Before she is even technically a mother, the Mistress is 'Herethical'. She is an outsider, but she is connected intimately to the relationships she is part of. There will be a marriage, or a long-term partnership between two people (who may also be parents) who are joined romantically and sexually, to which she is a party. What she does, and how she does it, and how she wears her joys and her sufferings, will alter the fate of these people. If she is not as discreet as she should be, if she is seen where she should not be, if she does not ensure that remnants of her bodily fluids are washed from the body of her lover post-sex and if she does not endure this desecration quietly, there is potentially the destruction of a marriage. This washing must also not be too vigorous, for as the (genderless) Mistress narrator (a rare gift indeed) of Jeanette Winterson's *Written on the Body* writes, this can also be a giveaway: 'I am informed by the thin glossy pages that the way to tell if your husband is having an affair is to check his underpants and cologne. The magazines insist that when a man finds a mistress he will want to cover his prick more regally than of old. He will want to cover his tracks with a new aftershave.'[19] Such a slip could change the fortunes of family, and possibly her own relationship with her lover. In short, the stable pregnancy of the situation relies upon her sexual kindness and often also, like with mothers, relies on her not receiving it in return. The fate of others is intimately tied to her sexual expression. The Mistress is a heretic, and therefore, a perfect mother, just like Sugar.

Get the fuck down, girl

A Mistress could also become pregnant and, in being so, has the ability to make and re-make worlds. For example, this could be a new world where her lover leaves his wife/family, or she could leave the relationship with her lover. No one could leave, yet the world will never be the same again. All these possibilities haunt the relationship. In Charlotte Brontë's *Jane Eyre*, Jane becomes both a Mistress and a Mother both to the child she has with Mr Rochester and Adèle Varens, the daughter Mr Rochester had with one of his former Mistresses, the opera dancer, Céline (though there is some doubt over whether he is the father). Here, Adèle represents the ever-present possibility of the Mistress becoming a mother, of fucking things up. In Jane, we also see the possibility of the Mistress as healer (even in relation to Mr Rochester's eyesight), of putting things right, but also of requiring men to do the 'right thing'. Such demands cannot be made lightly, though, as we saw with the tragic, pregnant, sexy and sexualized Lola, played by Scarlett Johansson in Woody Allen's *Match Point*.[20] The moment Lola becomes pregnant, she transitions from being the mysterious, very Marilyn Monroe, Mistress (compared to the neat, rich, overtly maternal, wifely wife), to a pain in the butt, and ultimately, dead. Pregnant Lola is shot by her pseudo-intellectual married lover, who – shock-horror – gets away with it. Sadly, the fate of the Mistress is often tragically sealed by the otherworldliness of her power. Of course, she might have the baby, and remain a Mistress, just as the real-life Elizabeth Smart. She could also be forced to have the baby when she does not necessarily want it since it was the result of rape, like enslaved Mistresses such as Sally Hemmings, who we met in Chapter 1, and whose story was revealed by the revolutionary enslaved Mistress, writer Harriet Jacobs.[21] She could become a mother after she has been a Mistress and when she is a wife, like Jane Eyre, or Joanna in *The Cry*. The possibility of cis women Mistresses to have children is often used as a way to both sexualize and control. Returning to Atwood's *The Handmaid's Tale*, we see that it is a matter of life or death whether a child is produced by the Handmaid. And then we see that in various states in the United States, particularly in the south such as Alabama, Arkansas and Arizona, there are constant threats to erode women's reproductive autonomy. *The Handmaid's Tale* feels more real, every day.

This particular aspect of the 'logic of misogyny' is especially reserved for heretical women, as Kate Manne argues in *Down Girl* – good mothers should be celebrated on earth and will be rewarded in heaven, while as to those who seek abortions, heaven is too good for them. Such women are an abomination.[22] This will all sound familiar to the Mistress. She is in a tight bind, since she may indeed not want to have the child, but if she does, she will not receive the same financial support as a wife might receive, especially if the parties to the birth are working class; nor will she receive the same emotional support that a wife might receive. Worse, she will herself be seen as a pariah for having the child, with the child a living embodiment of her 'sin'. If she does not want a child, she will be seen as falling again within the typical Mistress archetype of sexual but not maternal, and if she cannot have a child (due to an explained or unexplained fertility issue), then this will be seen as her fault, god's retribution, for ruining her womb. For Black women, particularly in the UK and US, childbirth is a risky business, full stop. For Black women there is an increased risk of death during childbirth, in addition to stereotyping.[23]

Trans women, particularly Black trans women,[24] by virtue of their non-cis status and not being able to give birth themselves, are then likely to be seen as 'other, other' women. This means they are hypersexualized both in respect of being trans and being Mistresses, and regarded as not deserving of rights as human beings, let alone the sexual kindness that all Mistresses are denied.[25] Motherhood, as it is currently construed, fucks over all women, one way or another, and doubly fucks the Mistress. Its power to profoundly alter worlds, as well as create them is not necessarily in its physical action, rather the power is vested in being the 'other, other' woman – forcing the world into seeing how it is to have your fate tied to another, but also how it feels for the world not to see *their* fate, as being similarly tied to yours. Sexual kindness, however, knows we are conjoined. This is Mistress Ethics.

One classy piece of sugar

Both Sugar and Jane Eyre have something in common, in that their beginnings were 'common'. Jane Eyre, although later employed as a governess, was an orphan. Sugar also became a governess, but began life modestly, in the seediest of Victorian London's brothels. It is made clear at the start of *Crimson Petal* that Sugar's friend and co-worker has been injured by a client, and there are constant references to disease and squalor in and around the brothel, almost to the extent of caricature. Although now I am privileged to write for a living, I too was a working-class Mistress. When I was eighteen, one of my lovers left his wife and we lived in a caravan with mushrooms growing through the floor and on the walls. It was rotten through and through. It was rare that we had enough to eat (tuna from a can and a mouldy donut for lunch was a favourite), which was usually because he gambled and drank away the small amount of money we had. People were often stabbed or shot on the caravan site, and every night, the air was thick with men shouting at their partners. Sometimes it was us, sometimes not, because I had become an expert at walking on eggshells. I remember being at a pub and running away from my lover, with a £20 note damp and sweaty in my clenched fist. I ran hard, and for my life. I can still hear my feet smacking the pavement. It was the last £20 we had and I wanted to be able to get the bus to work. It was worth the shit I would get for it later, because it was not just the bus ticket I needed, I needed my ticket out of there. Out forever, away from him. I was an eighteen-year-old hungry black-eyed white working-class Mistress, firmly in the closet, dreaming my way home. I hungered hard for escape, which sometimes took the form of a man.[26]

In *My Dangerous Desires*, lesbian sex radical, ex-hooker, incest survivor, poor-white trash, high-femme dyke Amber Hollibaugh tells stories of not feeling at home. Like Amber, who learnt fearlessly to grab hold of her identities, my early response to men who sniffed out that sugar was to become exactly what they feared (and wanted): an 'alarming, hazardous, sexually disruptive woman'.[27] At sixteen (although sixteen is the age of consent in the UK, I was still a minor for the purposes of the law. The age of consent is eighteen in the US), I was a whore. The wife of the 42-year-old man (who was the father of a close school friend) who sniffed out my vulnerability told me so. I learnt very early that what men did to their Mistresses and all the consequences that follow are because of what those Mistresses do, or allow to be done to their bodies. I learnt to give 'professional' blow jobs: a compliment the very same man gave me, while imploring me not to become the 'village bike'. The praise felt good, and home felt as though it was within reach. When the affair became gossip, I would see them everywhere I went in that shitty small town, either talking behind my back (loud enough that I could hear their whispers) or sometimes they would come up to me and shout it in my face. The witch hunt is what I now call it. What I have to understand, and I wish that every Mistress whose story intersects with mine understands too, is that what they beat and hound is not your sexuality but that *sugar*, that sexual kindness that is so terrifying to the world at large. Like Hollibaugh, my sexuality (in my case, my bisexuality) did not have space to emerge yet. Because I saw myself as a 'master of receptivity' and heteronormative romance, I could not see myself as anything other than fiercely straight, and forever in competition with other women.[28] It was not until I saw the possibility for my own sexuality to be other than in relation to men, that I could be the recipient of sexual kindness as well as the giver, that I could 'tune in' to another the love for women that, to society, can be so threatening because of its erotic revolutionary power.

What would god say?

Dolly Parton's hymn to the quintessential Mistress whom we all know, the ravishing woman called Jolene,[29] who may take your man without thinking twice, can make us feel a lot. The song can make us frantically search for the Jolene that we know, who might be getting ready to take our man, or it might make us breathe in relief that she has not entered our lives, yet. Or perhaps, you *are* Jolene. But is it really so, that she takes him, when actually, your man just wants a Mistress and, as history has proven to be his habit, takes her? It can't be helped. Such a resignation can be read in queer Black working-class Celie's laments of the mysterious Sugar (Shug) Avery's return, in Alice Walker's epistolary *The Colour Purple* which is compiled of Celie's letters to god, which are written in her own voice and African American Vernacular.[30] She laments her return because she knows her husband will want Shug and will take her as a Mistress, but she also knows that she will also fall in love with her. In fact, she wants her bad, as she writes in one of her letters. She wants her, and she says she does, explicitly to god, her judge: 'All the men got they eyes glued to Shug's bosom. I got my eyes glued there too. I feel my nipples harden under my dress. My little button sort of perk up too.'[31] When, through typical sexual kindness, Shug helps Celie discover her clitoris, there is a hot scene and a taboo-smashing line about the sexual rush Celie got from a breastfeeding, which she compares to the shiver she gets from touching her 'button' for the first time:

> I look at her (Shug) and touch it with my finger. A little shiver go through me ... She say, while you looking, look at your titties too. I haul up my dress and look at my titties. Think bout my babies sucking them. Remember the little shiver I felt then too. Sometimes a big shiver. Best part about having the babies was feeding em.[32]

Celie's letters to god are also a brave and powerful testimony against purity culture, particularly Christian purity. The concept of purity has been violating women since the philosophical and theological genesis of the concept centuries ago, and continues to perpetuate racial, sexual and spiritual violence.[33] Mistresses, like Celie, in their profound connection with the erotic, live a life that is de facto impure since their relationships are both outside of marriage and, in Celie's case, outside of straight sex. Celie's letters are Herethical text, reminding those that would listen that god loves Mistresses.

Celie knows her new husband, Mister, whom she never wanted to marry, wants Shug, and she masturbates thinking about them fucking in the room next door. 'But when I hear them together all I can do is pull the quilt over my head and finger my little button and titties and cry.'[34] Shug begins a sexual relationship with Celie, and through Shug (who is also married, to Grady), Celie discovers what it feels like to be wanted and cared for sexually and romantically, and to feel at home. She receives sexual kindness from her Mistress and by being a Mistress. Celie discovers the sexual kindness that *she wants*. It is extraordinary that she does, and through her sexual awakening, and the sexual kindness exchanged between the two women, she discovers her own power. As a consequence, Celie leaves her abusive husband, and Shug too. Shug returns to Celie many years later, to be with Celie as her partner. Mistress-hood for Celie is about getting home to herself, and knowing when she should have received sexual kindness. Mistress-hood is an identity that encompasses the vastness of sexual self-discovery, trauma, jealousy, recovery, healing and the desire to heal others. It is about hope and possibility for a better, kinder, hotter, hornier, world. The power of *The Colour Purple* is also in its unapologetic writing of Black working-class sexuality and queerness, as well as the fearless writing of what it means to experience sexuality amid trauma. Its power is clear, in its unpalatability – it is one America's most frequently 'banned' books.[35] A huge part of its power (and a reason also as to why it provokes revulsion) is because the novel allows the Mistress to tell her own tale, in her own voice.

A girl in every port

The Mistress lives in a secret world, either by choice or because she cannot disclose her Mistress status (for a whole galaxy of reasons ranging from threats from her lover or those close to them to the judgements she will receive from those close to her). To understand more about what keeps her world secret, we must understand more about *who* asks her to be kept secret: the husbands, wives and partners who are her lovers. I feel a jolt as I, and as I ask you to, shift perspective. I'm scared, because as we embark on this part of our journey, we must confront some considerable power, and retain the coherence of our story, and sexual kindness, in the face of centuries worth of assumptions, abuse and entitlement backed by law, backed by colonialism, patriarchy, cis-normativity and heteronormativity.

In the story of *Mrs Wilson*, Alison Wilson discovers that she is not the only Mrs Wilson, upon the death of her husband. Her husband, novelist and MI6 Agent Alec Wilson has many wives as Mistresses.[36] Upon Alec's death, we hear stories which see Alison's identity shift, from wife to Mistress. With that shift, we see her struggles with Alec's 'lawful' wife and family, who no longer recognize her right to her husband's body, and even to her memories as she believed them to be. We see her fabricate a version of the (clearly fraudulent) decree absolute that Alec had shown her as 'evidence' of divorcing one of his wives, all those years ago when she agreed to marry him. The conversations between the women as they are revealed to one another show the depth of deception, and the depth of each of their unreciprocated kindnesses towards Alec as (unwitting) Mistresses. And so too, the law is revealed as much more than a piece of paper – an instrument that ensures that both wives and Mistresses are punished by the proprietorship with which it endows roving husbands. Alison's sons jovially reminisce about their father and make the joke that he had a 'girl in every port'. Usually Alison would have brushed off such a joke, but having just discovered her husband's array of Mistresses, and her own sudden transition from wife to Mistress, from respectable woman to one of the girls in the many ports available to her husband, she rebukes them both. It is a rebuke that is not only about her own situation but also targeted towards an attitude – that men who have Mistresses are just being, well, men, yet she has now become a whore. Breaking the conventions of monogamy is always a male privilege.[37]

We are all familiar with these kinds of narratives, but what we are hopefully now coming around to is the idea that these stories are the stories we expect to hear, and nothing like the full story that exists in the hearts of many Mistresses across time and space. This multiplicity of stories will share common elements, and these common elements will be exactly the same every time: the law will set the Mistress apart, and her sexual kindness may, or may not, be abused in relation to her outsider status, and because of any factors that cause her to be additionally marginalized, such as race, gender identity, sexuality and class. So is the person who has a Mistress unkind, or is it actually the law which is unkind? The answer is both. But, the person who has a Mistress *always* has the power to give the Mistress sexual kindness.

The power of the cuckhold

The reason for much of this incredulity is that the Mistress in her taboo breakage becomes property, which is out of control, and therefore beyond control.[38] She's gone rogue. But the story does not stop with her; the legacy of being a Mistress is that it becomes an intergenerational 'stain'. Everyone, I am sure, has a mysterious aunt who remained unmarried but had a close married 'friend'. And oh gosh, she had a baby with a man out of wedlock. It can be a romantic stain too. The man who gifted me *Grand Central Station* is a fine example. After being manipulated into divulging my entire history, I revealed my Mistress past. This resulted in my being named untrustworthy, non-maternal and, actually, disgusting. Giving sexual kindness to the Mistress is about resisting ideas of property and control, and connecting with the pain that it is to fall in love as a secret. It is about love for the woman who puts herself in this exposing position, and caring for the whole of her that is exposed. Martin tells the story of Michelle, who has an affair with married Delia, who recounts this 'shroud of secrecy and shame' that prevented her from being with the one she loved, or even talking about the relationship.[39] Being a secret causes pain, and this requires acknowledgement, respect and kindness, not punishment. Subversion of this need to punish could also come in the form of the dynamic between the cuckhold husband and his 'hot wife', whose sexual kindness extends to recognizing that her desire for pleasure outstrips his, and therefore ought not be confined to notions such as fidelity. As Martin writes, such a recognition is so powerful that it could take him 'everywhere'.[40] Responsibility for reciprocation of sexual kindness to the Mistress means reading the other story, her story, and seeing the Mistress how we should: not untrue and troubled, as the old story would have us believe, but as, thoroughly, true.[41] Especially if she is *your* Mistress.

Power keeps Mistresses

It is likely that if you have a Mistress, you will hold power. It might be that you use your power well and kindly, and that you give to your Mistress and receive from your Mistress sexual kindness as it should be given and received. But it is also possible, and dare I suggest, likely, that you do not, and this is because of everything that has come before in this book: assumptions, distortions, lack of understanding and the need for the Mistress to be secret property. It is also likely that you have stopped reading by now, if this is you. But if not, great to have you here, and let's get uncomfortable. Let us look to the examples that have been set for how Mistresses have been had, kept and taken. To do this, we will need to get right up in the faces of the rich and powerful, the political and the philosophical.

The Personal I: The Mistress of the political

As early feminists told us, and many women remind us, daily, the personal is political. And this is something that is denied by those in power; it is almost as though the personal is the Mistress of the political. Donald Trump. Henry VIII. Such powerful men and those like them have benefited from laws and rules which support ownership and the control of property, which we know to be at the heart of how and why Mistresses can be deprived of the sexual kindness they deserve. Slavers such as Thomas Jefferson, who abused enslaved Mistresses like Sally Hemmings, were even protected by law, and of course many powerful white lawmakers and citizens at the time. Donald Trump has continually denied his numerous rumoured affairs throughout his three marriages. Perhaps the most famous Mistress of his is Stormy Daniels. Trump is rumoured to have had an affair with her during his marriage to Melania Trump, a year after he married her. Trump has continued to deny his affair with Stormy, despite various vindications of her story (and many other stories throughout his single term of presidency which he has continued to deny, seemingly without consequence). The secrecy is aggressive, and rationalized because it is a 'personal matter', and not anyone's business.[42]

We need not look back too far in time for another famous episode: Mistress Monica Lewinsky and married president, Bill Clinton, or otherwise the scandal known as 'Monicagate'. Again, the president's persistence at maintaining secrecy in the face of blinding evidence to the contrary, which led him to being held in contempt of court via the Paula Jones harassment case, was extraordinary.[43] Some of us will remember Clinton's famous 'I did not have sexual relations with that woman', which was broadcast the world over.[44] As I have mentioned above, Lewinsky gifted Clinton a copy of Baker's beautifully sexually kind *Vox*. This shows that Lewinksy is our archetypal Mistress. She gives sexually kindness but does not receive it. What she does receive is persistent secrecy, objectification (reduction to the 'woman who sucked off the President') and the exertion of power and control. In a similar vein, there is Boris Johnson, whose Mistresses have included lawyer Marina Wheeler, who later became his wife – that is, until subsequent and overlapping affairs came to light in the form of his Mistresses, writer Petronella Wyatt and journalist Anna Fazackerley.[45] There are no doubt many others, and yet, Johnson's power and influence remain undisturbed, and the relationship between his power and his keeping-secret (to varying degrees of success) of his Mistresses, unexamined. Yet a Mistress will be endowed with a lifetime stain of disbelief, since she is an 'adulteress'. I would like to be clear here that the fact of being in a relationship with a Mistress is not the issue; rather, the issue is with the quality of power that allows for the keeping-secret, and sometimes abuse, of Mistresses without damaging consequences, in fact, the opposite.

According to Kate Manne's *Down Girl*, moral and social labour tends to be publicly directed towards women and not men. This is exactly what happens to Mistresses. Negative and punitive consequences are deployed publicly to women who fall from their 'responsibilities' as 'good women', thereby ensuring such behaviour remains 'bad', as are those who might be tempted to support her.[46] Think of Mistresses you know, or know of – how do you feel when you think of them? I have been many times a Mistress and experienced all the sanctions, publicly too, but still, when I hear about a Mistress, I must work to wade through this logic of misogyny. Make no mistake, though, this logic, and this punishment, is absolutely designed to protect and maintain those in power, that is, those who have Mistresses. Not only will she be punished for falling from the logic but she won't be able to maintain her place in power – don't ask for in return what you give.[47]

It is powerful men that are more likely to have Mistresses, and who are also, more likely to be abusers of their power, and also their

Mistresses. It is men who are more likely to have Mistresses, because they are more likely to live within and aspire to masculine-coded perks and privileges such as social positions of leadership, authority, money, social status, prestige, along with pride, standing, reputation and importantly in the context of Mistresses – the absence of shame and public humiliation (or otherwise the absence of conventionally feminine moral labour).[48] Such power can often go hand in hand with abusive narcissism, which is built on a sense of entitlement to women and their sexuality, as property to be owned, and to be punished (physically, emotionally, psychologically), when she falls from the ideals that men believe 'their' women must attain and maintain.[49]

It is important to understand that figures with power such as Trump, Clinton and Johnson, whom I have mentioned, and John F. Kennedy, whom I have not, tend to think of themselves above the law, and therefore above and outside of these kind of logics.[50] It is possible, though, to hold power, and to hold a Mistress (as opposed to keep her). Holding a Mistress recognizes, and attempts (of course, with varying degrees of success), to be reciprocal in sexual kindness *outside* of logics, prejudices and structures which dictate the terms of the relationship. It is possible; I've been there when it has happened. I've received sexual kindness in this way, from a powerful man. Such men are prepared to be transformed rather than assert control – they are prepared to hold, and not have, and to give as well as receive. They are not scared of a woman's extraordinary capacity to receive pleasure, her natural voracious desire, her joyful, rageful, generous and persistent fight against that which contains her, and her profound connection with the erotic which exist between her and other Herethical women. He might even fight alongside her for Mistress Ethics.

The Personal II: The Mistress of the philosophical

Philosophers are no better than politicians. In fact, they might be worse, since they are the ones who gave coherence to the logic that gives the powerful their power. So, now it is the moment to do some philosophy, or rather, some philosophers. In a documentary about his life, French philosopher Jacques Derrida said he would love to hear other philosophers such as Immanuel Kant, Georg Wilhelm Friedrich Hegel and Martin Heidegger talking about their sexual lives. Derrida says their philosophies make these men appear 'asexual', and that he would love to hear them speak about the part that love plays in their lives, which is something they refuse to do.[51] He asks a huge question (although he resists answering it himself) – why have they erased their private life from their work? I think Derrida senses the threat of the Mistress, and the uncovering of the philosophers' secrets.

If the Mistress wanted to rely on an experienced philosopher for advice on how to construct her ethics, to whom should she turn? Will it be Heidegger, whose Mistresses were his Jewish students Hannah Arendt and Elizabeth Blochmannm, and who kept his wife appraised of his numerous affairs over several decades?[52] Kant was a notorious racist believing (and theorizing) race as a scientific category, but also in racial hierarchy, thereby giving philosophical credence to eugenicist science.[53] He also believed that sex and sexual desire would divert us from doing what is 'right' since it is threatening to our morality and rationality.[54] Of course, he means *his* (male) sexual desire. He also presupposes that morality and rationality are healthy concepts to use in thinking about sex and relationships. As to Sartre, at least he was able to acknowledge his thinking that sexual desire aims to capture the other's freedom; perhaps he was theorizing more from experience than he acknowledged in his philosophy.[55] As to Hegel, the architect of the 'master-slave' dialectic, as far as he was concerned, women belonged in the home and to the family.[56] Returning again to Heidegger, a philosopher fixated on essence, who had a problematic start to his career with membership of the Nazi party, he went on to write some of the heaviest and most complex philosophical texts ever written. I would be terrified as his Mistress – my admiration for Hannah Arendt in this regard extends to this, as well as for her razor-sharp impressive body of philosophy. It is interesting how Mistresses are inclined towards philosophy, and yet they rarely are regarded as philosophers. Any advice from the Western philosophical canon, or indeed any other of these (now dead) white men endowed with intellectual power, the 'heterophilosophical patriarchs',[57] is likely to be designed to talk over the Mistress.

Philosophers against consent

Simone De Beauvoir was both wife and Mistress to Jean Paul Sartre – she was his wife by virtue of their long-term bond, and Mistress to his bonds with others. She also kept her own Mistresses. It is interesting, too, that it is much easier to read of De Beauvoir's personal life, before one reads her philosophical ideas. In reaching this personal aspect to her philosophy, one will encounter a complex web, which includes the ill-treatment of her Mistresses. Of particular note, though, is the collective philosophical attitude within this continental, rather lascivious, oeuvre of which she was part, to one of the only laws that (albeit quite badly) might protect the Mistress. Along with Derrida, Louis Althusser, Foucault and Deleuze and Guattari, De Beauvoir signed a petition seeking the abolition of France's consent laws in 1977.[58]

There are many problems with modern consent law, some of which I have considered in the first chapter concerning how being legally able to consent depends on being considered as more than a form of property kept by power. The way that consent law is used and interpreted in US and UK courts causes re-traumatization of victims of sexual offences and causes survivors to be reluctant to engage in the legal process.[59] Judith Herman writes in her landmark text on trauma, *Trauma and Recovery*: 'Women quickly learn that rape is a crime only in theory; in practice the standard that constitutes rape is not set at the level of women's experience of violation but just above the level of coercion acceptable to men. That level turns out to be very high indeed.'[60] There are also problems in that consent sets a 'low bar' for sexual relationships, as agreement, rather than enthusiastic desire and want. Consent law also actively misses coercive elements in sex, meaning that rape can be perceived, or misunderstood, as consensual sex, resulting in severe and intergenerational trauma for victims.[61] It is also the case that the criminal justice system is constructed to facilitate abuse and, instead of remedying harm through community acknowledgement of the violence, retraumatizes survivors.[62] Consent is also rooted in colonialism and property, meaning that these ideas are further entrenched, often in the name and cause of white feminism and ultimately the preservation of systems that give power to the privileged.[63] Yet, although not perfect, it is what we have. At least it tries, albeit imperfectly, to safeguard against abuse of power, which, curiously, receives no mention in the petition, which, given their respective powerful positions, is to be expected. The philosophers' most persuasive point is one that they purposely miss: that the law on consent would never have believed *their* Mistresses, nor seen *their* abuses of power. In the late 1970s when this was happening, it would have been highly unlikely that Mistresses would have felt empowered, or have the outlets available, to tell their stories; even less so than now. This is why an argument can be made against consent: it does not protect, nor set a standard for protecting, those who are actually harmed. This is why sexual kindness must be much more than consent.

Given how the system is run and who is part of the system, consent and the criminal justice system protects the already powerful. To clarify, the issue is never one of consensual, sexually kind relationships with Mistresses, but rather, the persistent protection of power, which allows the continued concealment of the stories of Mistresses. Philosophers claim authority over thought, radical ideas and intellectual power, which allows them to disregard the experiences of others. The stories of Mistresses are formative of Mistress Ethics; not De Beauvoir's feminism, nor Foucault's philosophy, nor Heidegger's existentialism.

Mistress #MeToo

When Mistresses have broken the code of silence and spoken out about relationships where they have been abused, how have we received them? As I have said above, white women, particularly white middle-class straight cis women, tend to claim victimhood as their own, to the exclusion of others. Given that the Mistress is in direct opposition to the logic that gives these women such a power,[64] it is not a surprise that she receives a hostile reaction. There is a perception that since the sex that a Mistress has is de facto 'wrong', she cannot ever be in the 'right', or otherwise cannot be a victim of abuse, since she 'asked for it' in angering the logic. Or that she must be a slut, and basically who cares. This is absolutely the reaction I have received from some (not all) who have known about my Mistress relationships. I made my bed, so I must lie in it. And this includes passively receiving rape, psychological and emotional abuse, as well as physical abuse (from both married lovers and their partners). And this is my queer white working-class woman's experience. When we deign to hear the stories of Black women, women of colour and trans women, we find multiple layers of abuse and centuries of intergenerational trauma at the hands of colonial sexist laws designed to protect power and whiteness, at all costs.[65] If you have a Mistress of colour, please, for the love of Mistresses, do your anti-racism work. This is the minimum you must do for the privilege of her company.[66]

As I said at the start of this chapter, this shit is personal – it must be, since this is where the stories lie, both of complicity in the power that keeps Mistresses and stories of and by Mistresses. The personal is power; this is why political and philosophical power guard it fiercely and why the Mistress is deprived of her story. Because of that, I want you to begin to think about your story and whether, and how, Mistresses and Mistress-hood feature within it (or might come to feature in it). This next set of bullet points is therefore specifically addressed to *you*, and asks you to carefully and temporarily occupy the Mistress's body as she sits in her silence. Let this be an act of sexual kindness, which asks you to do what you thought was impossible, something both revolutionary and Herethical – imagine your fate, your suffering, your joy and hers are conjoined.

- You are a woman and you love a married woman. You know that the stakes are high if your relationship is found out; not only do you suffer the shame and ensuing witch hunt by virtue of having a relationship with a married woman but you're outed as loving women. It could be that hers or your race and/ or religion make this even more dangerous; perhaps it puts her in danger of violence, or perhaps it is a matter of life or death. Because you need to protect yourself, you need to live two lives: one in secret, and one in the open, but not free. Your capability of doing so indicates a problem to be pathologized.

- Money is tight. But you want to see your lover, and you know that hotel rooms are the only way. Your lover lives a long train journey away, which you cannot afford. It's the end of the month and you are running out of money. You have no savings. He doesn't understand, can't understand, what this means. You want to ask your lover for help, but you are scared of him. You're not quite sure why. You're scared that immediately you ask, he will end the relationship. Or worse, he'll think you are not good with money, or you only want him for money. You apply for a high interest dodgy pay-day loan. You keep doing this, time after time, and after a year, the repayments are now more than your salary.

- You are the lover of a powerful man. A president, perhaps. You know that when you are together, it's glorious. You have a room all of your own, with only him inside; it's everything you wanted. It reminds you of a story, a story in which two lovers are as if in a jar of their own – little figures to watch as if in a dolls-house brothel. They play out a story of intimacy and being at ease with one another. it's a spacious and kind story. *Vox* it is called, and you gift it to him, as you see that sexual kindness as a home in which you both live. Later, your relationship is exposed. You see the book you gave to him, thrown in the corner of his office, the dolls-house brothel smashed, your home burnt to ashes of denial and contempt. No one else will mourn it apart from you, sinner. Your animal shriek of pain can be heard by the waiting press who'll use it as front-page news, as the witch hunt begins.

- As a Black woman, you are viewed by white people as being able to withstand more. Mistresses are hurt daily, but as a Black Mistress, hell, you can take much more! No, you say, it is that I am *forced* to take more. Because you won't fucking listen. 'Exhaustion' is not even the word. Because of the colour of your skin, you'll be given your own stereotypes to reclaim, along with your own sexuality.[67] When you're outed as a Mistress, you know what will come and it'll be the white women that are among the worst. Your pain will be invisible twice. The Mistress is thought of as strong, because of the 'lifestyle' she chooses; you are thought of as strong not because of who you are, and your revolutionary power and the revolutionary power of your sexuality, but because of racist ideas that you do not suffer pain. Revelation of your Mistress status is risky for you. The things you do to keep being a Mistress secret, to keep both yourself safe from racism and your relationship safe, will be held as evidence of your 'duplicity'. Your white lover won't understand, because he doesn't know what it is like to be a Black woman. He won't have read those 'dangerous' books; he won't have walked a mile in your shoes, since he only lays in bed with you a couple of hours a day.

- You are a trans woman. The threat of your gender history being revealed along with your Mistress status is terrifying. It is with you every time you are with your married lover. There is just this feeling, lurking beneath the surface of your consciousness. And there's the thing he says about not liking 'queers' that give the hint of a shape to that feeling. You've never felt comfortable to talk to him properly. You laugh together often. He makes you feel good, and the sex is amazing; although there was that one time... You go out on the town, very late at night, and he enjoys how other men look at you. He enjoys the secrecy, and the thrill of the possibility of getting caught. He's a powerful man.

- They wrote a song about you, begging you not to take their man. You never understood it because you've never taken any man. They come to you, because they can sense your virtue. The question is always whether they will abuse you for it or not. Either way, it will be your fault if they do. And if they don't, then you will just be that weird woman who might be having an affair with that handsome powerful man because you are living out your fantasies of being a rich girl. Damaged goods.

- You are a young Jewish woman, you're are in a disgraceful affair,[68] with two well-known and powerful intellectuals. You're abandoned by both, at the start of Second World War, by letter. Your loss will never be understood, since it's not a loss in others' eyes, but a gain, since you are no longer living in sin.

- You love being a Mistress. You love the strangeness, the adventure, the romance and the pleasure. You love the survival. But the world wants you gone.

- You know you want children, and you want them with him. 'You are a manipulator', he said while holding you to him, for the most fertile years of your life. 'Because you enjoy sex, have had sex, you are no mother. Your desire is male. Not like my wife. She shows me every day that she is mine, that she belongs to me.' You want to leave him, but you love him, because of all the laughing and the joy. But now your sexual kindness is evidence of your 'bad character'. Though it's only sickness you feel these days; you are exhausted from arguing with him about who you are and what you feel. You are sick of being sick and tired. He has altered the structure of your body now. The abuse is so internalized that your flesh has changed. You fear it has made you infertile, except you don't think it's him, you think it's you.

Story Part III: There's a queer thought

There's that line of your hip, like the curve of a wet river, smelling of the same spices as your vulva. Some of those spices are in the Chai latte, which we both order since coffee makes us anxious. I say, 'I'm awkward anyway'; most bi girls are. 'Do we care for stereotypes?' I ask. She doesn't answer, only smiles and takes a sip of her Chai latte. She sits next to me and I'm forcing my eyes to stay in contact with hers; if they drop, they'll go one way: to her breasts. She makes me feel like a pervert. They're swelling, even beneath that loose black sweater she's wearing. She's what men would call 'pleasantly plump'. I call her 'fucking hot'. Marilyn is her name. As I watch her lips on her latte glass, I imagine them on various parts of my body. As I do, my clitoris hardens, and feels as though it extends out infinitely; far further than my lover's delicious cock, when it's in that desperate state I love. Marilyn gets all the guys, including the married man I'm seeing.

He's her husband. At the moment that hotel room door slides shut, his path changes from towards, to away, from me, and it's to her that he's drawn. When I am staring at the horrible screwed-up, screwed-up like my life, blue polyester bed runner, he's rushing back to her. I don't blame him for rushing. I would rush, too.

One day, I'd written an email to my lover. The problem was that she was using his laptop, and Marilyn saw the email. I don't know what happened after that; all I know is that my phone rang almost immediately after I had pressed send; it was his name on my phone screen. It felt like too urgent a call for it to be just him ringing to chat about the message I'd sent. Our relationship was joyously spacious, you see; there was a simple longing for one another and it was uncomplicated by a need to possess. It was extraordinary for that. I answered the call, and it was Marilyn. It's the moments like that, in a Mistress's life, that she dreads. The moment signifies the beginning of her execution: it signals the start of the witch hunt, and the moment her lover picks a side. He stays or he goes. I was more alone in that moment than I'd ever felt as I braced for the swearing, the insults, among which one word was inevitable. I closed my tear-saturated eyes tightly, and braced for 'slut' to ring its ancient toll in my ear. And for the cry that would follow, from my sex-positive friends, to reclaim this moment as my own.

Except – it never came. Of course, Marilyn was angry. Of course, I felt the expected hate in her words. But there was something else, too. Something glowed underneath them and I couldn't, yet, grasp at what it was. I'd stopped crying, and I'd stopped running.

She just asked me if I ever thought of her. I replied that, of course, I did. It's complicated. That was when it began, and how I ended up there, drinking Chai Latte, with you.

3

Fearing the queering: Bisexual, queer and kinky Mistresses

The queer Mistress duchess

In this chapter, I will be concentrating on that most fascinating of affairs, the most hot and mysterious – the one between a Mistress and wife. It is this affair that is, in many ways, the most compelling. It is not a relationship that one automatically thinks of either sexual or kind, but it is, in fact, both. This relationship is comprised of the full spectrum of colour that we saw glinting at us between Sugar and Agnes in Chapter 2, and it can be spectacular in its revolutionary power.

Sexual kindness in Mistress relationships can lead desire into directions that the straight, binary imaginary, does not expect. Take, for instance, Lady Bess Foster of Bath. She is a friend to the Duchess of Devonshire, Georgiana Cavendish, and Mistress to Georgiana's husband, the cruel Duke William Cavendish of Devonshire. The film

The Duchess is set in the eighteenth-century, and we see bisexual love and desire shape the story between the two women, the wife and the Mistress, in ways we would not expect generally, and certainly not for the time.[1] William is cold to Georgiana from the beginning, sexually distant and cruel. He takes Mistresses and does not hide them from Georgiana, which is just one form of cruelty he uses to punish her for not giving him the son and heir he covets and requires to maintain his bloodline. Georgiana befriends Bess at a party, and she soon moves into the marital home. Bess becomes William's Mistress, and Georgiana's pain is inevitable, but the pain she feels is not at William's betrayal (she is used to this, after all) but because he has taken Bess from her, 'the one thing I had of my own'.[2]

The two women quickly resume their friendship, and with that, things get hotter. Bess is in her nightgown, talking with Georgiana in her bedroom. The conversation turns to sex, and seeing Georgiana's distaste for it from her experiences with William, Bess tells her that it can, actually, be good. Bess starts touching Georgiana, and tells her to think about what she and Charles Grey, a handsome politician who has not hidden the fact that he is in love with Georgiana, might do together in the bedroom. Bess tells Georgiana to imagine how it would feel for him to touch her, while showing her what it means to be touched by someone kind. The scene is not just of Georgiana's sexual awakening but it is also the most powerful sex scene in a film that is really all about sex. The scene is symbolic of a deep sexual connection as Bess becomes the guardian and enabler of Georgiana's sexual freedom. Bess knows that this is a responsibility that will require sexual kindness from her, and this she delivers. Georgiana begins an affair with Charles Grey, and William is displeased since, of course, society has told him that he is entitled to lovers, and his wife must allow it and expect it. Her needs are irrelevant. Bess advocates for Georgiana's relationship with Charles, telling William that she is 'only asking of us, what we ask of her'. William is angry, and refuses to be a 'cuckhold'. Nevertheless, Bess helps Georgiana conduct the affair in secret, and even summons Charles for Georgiana knowing the personal risk that she herself takes should William find out – both she and Georgina would be in huge trouble. Georgiana becomes pregnant by Charles, and, aflame, William sends her away to the countryside to have the baby in shame, and to give the baby away to be brought up by Charles's family. Bess begs William not to go through with the plan, but he insists, acting as though he has no choice, both to stop the relationship between Georgiana and Charles but also to have Georgiana's child taken away from her. Since he will not change his mind, Bess asks that she is able to go away with Georgiana to tend to her while she has the child. William refuses, but Bess, now raging at the Duke, refuses his command and accompanies Bess. Bess is there with her, and through the desolation of Georgiana as her baby, Eliza, is wrenched from her arms. Bess holds her with such love, and such fury, against the terror of possession, marriage, monogamy and of hetero-sex gone wrong, the injustice of the containment of sexuality and motherhood, that it can only be sexual kindness. Beloved Bess: they were so scared of her.

By now, I think we can agree that the Mistress provokes fear. I think we can also agree that part of this fear is that the Mistress will take something that belongs to us, an idea that is rooted in colonialism, patriarchy and property. We also fear her because we are told to, and because we like to think of her as 'fallen', preferring to distance ourselves from her and her story, lest we also fall, which we inevitably will. There is a greater fear that underlies all of these though, and it is the fear that we will 'queer'. It is a fear that the Mistress will reveal that human desire, specifically women's desire, is and has always been resistant to the containers that it has been given.

For the love of June

Anaïs Nin and Bess share something. Sure, they share a husband with a wife. But they share something else, with each other – they share that they have a desire for women. In her diaries of her affair with Henry Miller and his wife, published as *Henry and June*, Nin tells us what it is like to hold desire as a Mistress. It is full and confusing: 'I hate June, and yet there is beauty. June and I melted together, as it should be. Henry must have both. I want both, too. And June? June wants everything; because her beauty demands it. June, take everything from me but not Henry.'[3] Anaïs is terrified of June, and Henry's persistent love for her, and June's love for him – likening June's love as a 'devastating tornado',[4] while their love remains deeply rooted. Nin laments the times Henry is in love with June, and seems to go away from her – yet Henry insists that it is a 'double flow', that one does not diminish the other. Nin's experience is not so linear, and nor is June's. There are echoes of Bess in June, for like Bess, Nin frees June to an inaccessible part of her, a self of her own, unreachable by Henry.[5] This space is also a sexuality of her own, a freedom, a madness, a kindness, that Anaïs awakens in her: 'We say, "Let us be sane with Henry, but together let us be mad."' Nin is a powerfully kind Mistress.

She is committed to the cause of understanding her sexuality, and sharing and writing these understandings, and her deliberations are as endless as they are arousing, touching at the very things that a Mistress confronts every day. Through doing this, she creates a space of sexual kindness in which she, and June, and Henry meet, secret from the world. Yet what might conventionally be understood as 'sexual consummation' between Nin and June is less clear, though it is strongly hinted at in the diaries, and certainly articulated in the 1990 film adaptation *Henry and June* by Philip Kaufman.[6] You can make up your own mind, but I see a far deeper affair, earth shattering, in fact, between Nin and June than I read between Nin and Henry. It was always June that she wanted. The affair is not just one of the body or the mind but of the world – between them, June and Nin carve another world for themselves in which to meet. They hold a space entirely for one another, one that is transient, open and infinite, yet faithful in that it excludes Henry, and perhaps, all men. It is tiny, in that it is concealed within each of them, yet it can unfold across oceans of time and space. It looks and feels as sexual kindness.

Let's get dirrrty!

In the opening of the first part of the volcanic *Grand Central Station,* it is all about Smart and Barker's wife. OK, it is Barker himself that causes her blood to 'spring to attention', but it is *her* that catches her eye: 'for after all, it is all her'.[7] And planted in the middle of this assault upon her by love, by him, who stumbles in her wake, is a tantalizing line as part of her many poetic metaphors: 'One should love beings whatever their sex, I reply but withdraw into the dark with my obstreperous shape of shame, offended with my own flesh'.[8] She knows that becoming a Mistress places her in a space of openness to sexual expressions that are (especially in the time of writing) condemned. Her story is one of rage, and of love, but again it is the story between Smart and Barker's wife, that causes those delicious soul tremors when you read it. There is striking similarity between Smart's account and Nin's – both of them ask the question of how to love *her*. Loving him has an air of inevitability about it, perhaps even banality. Barker is barely there, but for being the cause of Smart's pain.

The deeper ethical question in both stories is about love and desire, for and between Mistresses and wives, and the extent to which it transcends, overcomes and tells us where to find injustice. I want to be clear, though: a Mistress's desire is transformative not despite its filthiness but because of it. Smart's story is not one of intense physical sexuality with Barker's wife but it is desire nonetheless and certainly a story of sexuality. Even without explicit sexuality between wives and Mistresses, there is explicit sexuality, in the form of shared bodies. Find me a Mistress who has not stared at her lover's cock, got as close as she can, to see where his wife's juices might be hiding. Did they fuck this morning, or the previous night? It is an unbearable mystery – where do those traces go? Do they ever disappear? Can they be felt, even if the visible marks are scrubbed and soaped? If the light was ultra-violet, would it be possible to see his wife's hand prints on parts of him that you have claimed just for you? Could you see a saliva trail across that nipple, across that breast that you had taken refuge upon? Or that chest where you have made your home? Is her wife still there within the folds of her vulva?

When he showers after he has fucked you, do you turn away, when he washes his cock so that it no longer smells of you? Did he wash it well enough before he came to you? Something smelled different, yet delicious. It is funny how we forget, and how these traces can be washed away, and yet, a Mistress's shame will stick, even after she is burnt at the stake. The Mistress's sexual kindness demands that we must not look away.

Are all Mistresses bisexual?

In her famous piece *The Laugh of the Medusa*, Hélène Cixous writes, 'Everything will be changed once woman gives woman to the other woman.'[9] What she means is that the touch of the 'other' woman brings a woman home to herself, or gives her back to her body. In touching the 'other woman' she gives herself the space of sexual kindness that Nin and June gave to one another. The body of any woman, as we know, was never hers, since it belongs to man, to law, to gender, to marriage, to motherhood or anyone but her. In loving a woman, particularly a woman Cixous calls 'other', a woman finds this inaccessible space that June sought, that most Mistresses will have sought, perhaps even most women.

Love between women can generate the possibility for big changes, especially when this love comes from the 'other woman'. Other women love in other ways. For Cixous, other women are everywhere – she has a desire that gives, she comes in between herself, me and you, and she thrills in her becoming. She cuts through defensive loves, and 'she runs her risks'.[10] The Mistress is the Other Woman; we know this since it is a charge often thrown at Mistresses, as an insult, to indicate a status of second-best, less-than and other than the wife, other than the good. But, it is most certainly the other way around. Such a power resides in what Cixous suggests is universal bisexuality, which means not necessarily the desire for both (although it could of course mean this) but it means the collapsing of 'unitary' sexual identity into sexuality 'that does not annul differences, but stirs them up'.[11] There is no greater stirring, of loins, of blood, or rumours, of tempers and rage, than that brought by the Mistress. So, you must be asking yourself this by now: is the author of this book saying that all Mistresses secretly want to fuck the wives of their husband lovers? My answer is that sometimes yes and no, sometimes yes and yes. Sometimes yes, yes. Yes! But never no and no.

I am a bisexual woman (because I consider myself attracted to more than one gender) who has also often been a Mistress (predominantly to men). I am a proud bad dyke. I came out as bisexual in my mid-thirties, though it was not so much a coming out but a steady realization. Falling in love with women meant falling in love with myself and giving myself my own body and my own sexuality. My bisexuality is two things to me: a space of refuge, and a space of exposure, worry and vulnerability. As Meg-John Barker and Alex Iantaffi write in *Life Isn't Binary*, 'bisexuality' is a word for non-binary sexuality, and bisexuals comprise the largest group among the LGBTQ+ community, yet it is the sexuality that is most erased, and rendered invisible in popular and dominant cultures.[12] Sadly, bisexual people are also the most likely to feel suicidal, attempt suicide and experience anxiety and depression. They are also less likely to seek support or disclose their sexuality to healthcare providers.[13] Along with a lack of belonging, 'biphobia' persists with harmful stereotypes such as 'it's just a phase', not being able to decide, being greedy, or worse, unwilling to give up heterosexual privilege and being a promiscuous spreader of disease.[14] These stereotypes persist in both the straight and gay/lesbian communities. The difficult yet essential step we must take, according to Barker and Iantaffi, is hand in hand with Cixous. Barker and Iantaffi demand that the 'spectrum' or Kinsey scale is *not* enough. In fact, it is *harmful*. We need to stir up difference, cut through it and arrive at ourselves, again and again. We need instead to understand sexuality as fluid, and mappable – with locations and encounters changing across space and time. My own journey with my bisexuality has found me free a space for myself and my desire, but also the source of my deepest connection to women. Of course, I want to fuck them as well. It is a different kind of fucking, though, than my fucking with men. Fucking women feels like fucking for myself and for her; fucking men always felt like fucking for him. Fucking women, as a woman, is also a way of thinking, as well as doing and feeling. When I fuck her, I want to fuck her again. I want to keep coming, and so does she. With her, it is a desire that gives, and is without limit; it can reach across space and across time. It is ancient and right now. Sex with her is resplendent with those 'precipitous flights between knowledge and invention', and we are always creating. Fucking as a Mistress is precisely this. Ethically, Mistresses are always bisexual, for they are the other woman; universally bisexual, always undercutting difference, never stopping and carrying out the resistance that is their everyday lives, in and out of their bedrooms. They are creators of spaces of sanctuary, love and desire in and of itself, spaces of refuge that are inaccessible to those which would hurt us and those in power.

They are holders of secrets, which they are not afraid of. They are creators of spaces of sexual kindness, and these spaces are built by women to sustain and pleasure themselves, full of 'other women' – *In one another, we will never be lacking.*[15]

This is why I say that it is never a 'no and no' answer to the question, Are all Mistresses bisexual? As Mistresses, conventional ethics make no sense to us, because they are made for heterosexuality. Mistresses are always bisexual. Of course, they may or may not fancy men, and/or women, or any gender, or indeed anyone. They may not fancy the wife of their husband lover. It has not happened to me, though I have certainly fancied another Mistress of my husband lover. I can absolutely identify with the way that Nin and Smart write about the wives of their lovers, though. And perhaps even, it is a desire that is, or has been, perfectly sexual. Perhaps the sharing of a wife's husband has been my way of *coming close to her.*

Making kinky things happen

It makes sense that people are scared of Mistresses. They make waves, and this is no surprise because that's what love between women does. Audre Lorde said it. As does Sara Ahmed, who writes in *Queer Phenomenology* that the contingency of lesbian desire makes things happen.[16] Women desiring women fundamentally disorientates us, things, our lives. And then stuff happens. It queers us, since it makes us veer off the straight and narrow.[17] So it makes sense that we fear it and try to contain it: it's logical. Anti LGBTQ+ misogyny fits right in with the kind of malignant narcissistic power of the man who takes and has a Mistress.[18] It is part of that which maintains power, because women loving women threatens the possessory requirements of straight marriage; women loving women undermines power and access to women's sexuality by powerful men. And one thing we know about power, particularly power rooted in colonialism and patriarchy, is that it must have access to all areas. As Audre Lorde said, we are taught to suspect this profoundly erotic power, and so we do. And women have been made to suffer and have been rendered contemptible by virtue of its existence.[19] We know from Chapter 1 that the Mistress is in touch with the power of the erotic, because of her day-to-day engagement with this power. So, we suspect the Mistress, as we suspect her power. We suspect her power because it is erotic, and because it undermines misogyny through its connection to, ethical entwinement with, and love of, women. Her desire is by its nature kinky, which by its nature also shakes things up.

Mistress de Sade

Mistresses can be Mistresses of Kink. They can be dominant 'doms'; think 'yes, Mistress... ' They can be submissive 'subs', and they can spank, they can be spanked, they can fulfil fantasies – while dressed in leather. Kink is a way of fulfilling fantasies and satisfying desires, as well as being a space where sexual kindness happens. As Pompi Banerjee, Raj Merchant and Jaya Sharma, members of the *Kinky Collective* in India remind us, kink is a place of experimentation where politics and desire can combine. It is where we can question certainty and rationality, and instead move with doubt. Kink can root us ethically, so that the experimentation is consensual and instead of judgement, the *subversion* of judgement is essential.[20] This shows us that a Mistress of Kink might be uniquely placed to understand what sexual kindness might sound like when it is asked for as part of a conversation between consenting adults. In *Masochism: Coldness and Cruelty in Venus in Furs*, Deleuze asked the question as to whether Leopold von Sacher-Masoch and Marquis de Sade could be described as great 'clinicians' or experts on sexuality.[21] I think he was asking the right question, just of the wrong people.

For those new to such things, Leopold von Sacher-Masoch was the author of the novella *Venus in Furs*, and Donatien Alphonse François (Marquis de Sade) was the author of *Philosophie dans le Boudoir* ('Philosophy in the Bedroom'). The Marquis de Sade was a famously profane, quease-inducing, libertine author of books that depict violent sexual fantasies, as well as being a philosopher and French aristocrat. The link between these aspects of his identity might be well worth considering, but I shall not dwell on this here, save for referring the reader to the previous chapter; particularly the section 'Power keeps Mistresses,' onwards. For now though, let us hold the Marquis in our minds, as gently as we can. Leopold von Sacher-Masoch came along much later, with his less known *Venus in Furs* which reflects his fantasies to be submissive to dominant women. What Deleuze meant by the question he posed was not whether de Sade and von Sacher-Masoch were in any sense doctors or healers, but rather whether they might tell us something about the world through the way they document their sexual practices. This is indeed a useful idea, particularly in thinking about the Mistress.

Writing = Power

Deleuze found that in writing explicitly about sex, as these two authors do, there is a particular power given to the word that can communicate the physicality of a sexual experience more than other mediums – it can provoke the body into experiencing the sensations reported. He finds de Sade often employs obscene descriptions, whereas von Sacher-Masoch uses them rarely, instead preferring to leave the body within his literature to be in a state of indeterminacy – the body is always, tantalising, wrapped in furs.[22] It is interesting that von Sacher-Masoch's Mistress remains this way, and that she could never be given the power that de Sade held, to render explicit her body and her power. Of course, we have an interesting philosophical triad of power here, constructed by these three men, all three being powerful authors, writers and thinkers. As we understand this, it is important also to remember what Cixous wrote, that women have been reluctant to write about their desires; especially in the form that 'great men' have felt able to and have thereby dominated sexual expression: 'And why don't you write? Write! Writing is for you, you are for you; your body is yours, take it. I know why you haven't written … Because writing is at once too high, too great for you, it's reserved for the great-that is, for "great men."'[23]

Jeanette Winterson claims writing for the Mistress in *Written on the Body*, at the centre of which is a genderless Mistress narrator, who falls for the married Louise.[24] Through her prose, Winterson makes us wonder what the power of our bodies might be, if we were to find our own inner Mistress, rather than our master, 'it's a strange combination of mortality and swank, the all-seeing, all-knowing brain, *mistress of so much*, capable of tricks and feats. Spoon-bending and higher mathematics.'[25] This is not a 'mastery' – since in the narrator's language, the body does not become a master, but a Mistress. And all the more radical since we are asked to become Mistresses of our brains – an organ often separated from and not assumed to be the root of a woman's power. In understanding how to be kind to the Mistress, we understand that we must start questioning how our bodies are taken from us – with the restoration of her power, we find our own.

Won't you make me a Leatherdyke?

The kinky body written and painted in the works of de Sade and von Sacher-Masoch, does not belong to the 'other woman'. Deleuze's philosophically famous 'deploring of the orgasm' (that originates from his work on *Venus in Furs*) is not the creation of the Mistress – the idea is the creation of those who deplore her, whether they realize it or not. Deploring might not necessarily mean hate, but it is the deprivation of a space of her own, and her own possibilities. Fortunately, along came the Leatherdykes. A Leatherdyke is a queer woman who enjoys sadomasochistic practices. What seems clear from the literature I have seen from within this community (I am not a Leatherdyke, though I wish I was) is that there is something present within the community that is revolutionary: women talking about what turns them on, even if, especially if, it is considered outside the 'norm'.[26] Leatherdyke pioneer, Alex Warner, created an exhibit representing the diversity of the leatherdyke community and aims to create an ever-expanding archive of the experiences of the leather woman in all her glory.

Warner called the exhibition 'A Room of her Own'.[27] Other pioneers of this community such as Christine, the writer and artist founder of the leatherdyke Zine, FIST,[28] have also created spaces where women fuck, and write about fucking, as themselves and in whatever form it comes in the service of the Mistress's power, whether it is spanking, fisting, cutting, whipping, wax play, humiliation, rope play, restraints and maybe entering the 'subspace' (a euphoric state of flow experienced by submissives).[29] Kink generally (though not always) is considered a space where trans, gender queer/non-confirming, non-binary and gender-fluid people can feel more at home and able to express their sexuality, and basically, to fuck.[30]

The Mistress of Kink is therefore particularly powerful. Ethically, in accordance with BDSM codes, the sex she has will be subject to rigorous consultation, boundaries and negotiation, consent, discussion of aftercare requirements and, of course, discussion of what her desire requires. She therefore commands a space of sexual kindness where the rules are actually spoken and written. She speaks what is conventionally made unspeakable. She is also, however, in an ethical negotiation that exceeds this more obvious space of consent and negotiation, which is but a part of the expanse of sexual kindness the Mistress inhabits. What kinky sex does is show that giving voice to what could make sex kinder, to what we need, is possible. Talking about different risks, about sex, is possible. This is a crucial tool for the Mistresses, though it is not without its complications. The major complication is that the Mistress is always on the back foot, because her existence, sometimes literally in life or death terms, depends on her being secret, quiet, silent and, seemingly, compliant. She is often not on an equal footing with those who put her at risk, and is not necessarily a part of the kink community. Yet, the Kinky Mistress is an essential guide because she is prepared not only to talk and write her fucking but to place what feels good (and not so good) for *her*, her story, at the centre of her *own* ethics, in a sexual context that is outside of what is conventionally considered 'normal'. Kristeva would be delighted, since the Kinky Mistress is very much into Herethics.

Whores and Witches

As we know from Sollée's *Witches, Sluts, Feminists*, Witches have always embodied the sexual fears of men, whether it be these slutty women finding pleasure without them, or by emasculating or castrating them. The Witch/Mistress occupies a thin line for men, between disgust and arousal.[31] It is a familiar contradiction, and with the release of *Wet Ass Pussy* ('WAP') in August 2020 by Cardi B and Megan Thee Stallion, there was predictable uproar at the unapologetic, explicit and revolutionary expression of sexuality by two Black women.[32] It is a wild song which throbs with sexuality and joy. It is not a song to hear but to drink. Between two thighs. Of course, the uproar was mainly from men – most notably from one British white man who has a huge platform, and someone who has (by his own admission) taken multiple Mistresses – Russell Brand.[33] It was tiresome to hear him waxing on about WAP not being the revolutionary anthem women have claimed, since it follows the frame of masculine desire that women are supposed to be seeking to subvert through feminism. Of course, this assumes that desire belonged to men in the first place. Men have not heard women, because they have been scared of the witches, with their reactions being judgement, and sadly, punishment. It is left now to women to reclaim their desires, their stories, their philosophies and their touch; their rage and their sexual kindness. It is as though men like Brand are frozen, unable to take that leap toward giving sexual kindness to women, especially to women who rejoice in their sexuality, and especially to their Mistresses, if Brand's books are anything to go by.[34] This frozen state is a combination state – characterized by the listener and watcher of WAP, who is at once judgemental and aroused, poised to punish.

This is hard, like my clitoris, when I think of all those 'lesbian Witches' accused of seducing women, particularly 'naïve, unsuspecting wives'.[35] Sollée writes of one woman, or so-called 'lesbian witch' who was accused of witchcraft for fucking nuns with her tongue and strap-on.[36] The satanic sex such witches were described as having was always penetrative, with the women penetrating each other, or the woman penetrating a man. I like to imagine the (likely heterosexual) men who wrote these accounts about such 'disgusting women', with a secret hard-on and, so it seems, a pegging fantasy. It is hard to give kindness when one is in this judgement/arousal state, and this is the staunchest barrier to giving sexual kindness. Sexual kindness is a realm to which Mistresses are native and yet feels frighteningly alien to others. Yet it is a realm that exists tantalizingly close to us. In it you will also find all kinds of Mistresses – Sex Worker Mistresses, or 'Sacred Whores', Ratchet Feminist Mistresses, Mistresses twitching their tongues, between legs and within buttock valleys, across anuses and doing those revolutionary things – speaking and writing; casting their spells. There is alchemy within these stories.

The stories of Marilyn Monroe, Simone De Beauvoir and Anne Lister

When we learn about the stories of Mistresses, we also learn about gender, particularly about the ways we live gender, and the harm caused by our colonial violence of the gender binary. Marilyn Monroe, Simone De Beauvoir and Gentleman Jack might appear unlikely bedfellows, and yet they share common wounds. To explore how Mistresses help us understand more about gender, I am going to look at micro-snippets from the stories of these three Mistresses.

1. In the 1950s, actor Marilyn Monroe (often described as 'troubled') had an affair with the playwright Arthur Miller, who wrote such famous plays as *The Crucible*. They eventually married, and they remained married for five years. According to Abbott, Arthur Miller was quoted as saying that part of Marilyn's charm and magic and why she was a serial Mistress, was her ability to 'draw out the essential qualities of men'.[37]

2. Simone De Beauvoir's Mistress-hood is complex. She is both Mistress to Sartre, though they are in an open relationship and whether her involvement with him is ever unknown to his other lovers, long or short term, is unclear. Simone De Beauvoir has a Mistress, though, in Bianca Lamblin, her philosophy student. Lamblin also becomes involved with Sartre. De Beauvoir believed herself superior to her women

lovers, and other women in the lives of both her and Sartre.[38]
In her famous *The Second Sex*, she wrote that women dream
of achieving transcendence through love, and that through
this she can overcome the inferiority imposed upon her, yet
she gives up her own identity in the process.[39] Thus she writes
in a letter to Sartre: 'it is not only our relationship which you
have successfully established, it is really your life, your ethics,
and my own life by association.'[40] Her Mistress Ethics belong
to Sartre.

3. According to *The Secret Diaries of Anne Lister*, 'Gentleman
   Jack' (a name meant to taunt Anne Lister, by virtue of her
   appearance and sexuality) from whom apparently, in the
   tabloid imaginary, 'no woman was safe',[41] was Mistress to
   Mariana Lawton, who was married to Charles Lawton.
   According to her diaries, Mariana's marriage, and her sexual
   infidelity to Anne, was a great source of pain to her. The pain
   she experienced was physical as well as emotional, since Anne
   contracted venereal disease via Mariana's marital sex with
   Charles, who apparently had another Mistress in the form of a
   servant.[42]

By looking at how the gender binary impacts our assumptions
about Mistresses, we can understand more about both gender and
Mistresses. In Marilyn's story, we see a common assumption at play
– the Mistress gives a man what he needs. This feeds the idea that
men need to have Mistresses, and thus are entitled to them; which is,
of course, a function of the logic of misogyny that protects power.[43]

Beautiful Marilyn, who is often pathologized as mentally vulnerable, weak, soft and womanly, is framed as the ultimate Mistress, super 'womanly', and ultimately, less than male. It should not be a surprise to us that she is treated as such. De Beauvoir initially appears nothing like Monroe, but in fact, through her philosophy, she finds power in being almost exactly like her. She even accedes her ethics to Sartre's, through her philosophy and through her love, which become one and the same. She was, and she knew it, beholden to gendered assumptions as a Mistress, and somehow, even her taking of her own Mistress, Bianca (whom, if you read *A Disgraceful Affair*,[44] you will see she treated appallingly), comes through as not truly being for her (of course she shares Bianca with Sartre). Instead, she appears to accept that she will repeat the behaviour of the men in her life, and finds power in that. Yet that power causes harm to Bianca, her Mistress, and no doubt to De Beauvoir herself. In Anne's story, we can see the disturbing idea that in wanting sex and love that does not involve men, her pain is rendered invisible – both the pain she suffered and the harm caused by the husband in the story, Charles. The gender binary does no one justice in so many ways, and when we look to the Mistress, we understand yet another, and very particular, way. We can see from these stories (and there will be countless others untold) that the gender binary is foundational to the assumptions that cause pain to the Mistress. The stories recounted here demonstrate how well-told stories by well-known Mistresses conceal the structural and personal pain absorbed by virtue of being a Mistress. Nonetheless these stories are of cis gender white Mistresses. The stories are also of relatively powerful Mistresses. The stories of trans Mistresses, Black Mistresses, Mistresses of colour and working-class Mistresses will be at once more heart-breaking, and intentionally untold. Western society goes to great lengths to protect gender, and its marriages, and the cost is borne always by Mistresses despite what they give. Sexual kindness recognizes this, and makes reparation.

Mistress/Mx

As we know, I have always enjoyed, somewhat and increasingly reluctantly, the French mad/anarchic philosopher/psychoanalyst/ activist pair Gilles Deleuze and Felix Guattari's philosophy. There is something very Pastis in a dingy French café about this philosophical duo, who were particularly active after the 1968 academic protests in France. As we know from Chapter 1, the 'Body without Organs' is a 'layer' of our bodies, and it is capable of being more than one sex, n sexes, in fact.[45] This is also what is termed by Deleuze and Guattari, 'microscopic transsexuality'. This means that within our bodies, within the flesh that desires, is a power to be anything, and most importantly, to be anything, other than what we were told we must be. As a Mistress, I found this to be an empowering idea. Although I felt like I should be like Marilyn, I was nothing like her, and so I felt that I lacked worth, was less of a woman, because I wasn't. And so, I tried to be like De Beauvoir, but I wasn't like her either. I felt more like the genderless narrator from Winterson's *Written on the Body*.[46] Sometimes I felt like a man; or like I had a penis, anyway; like my arousal could extend in front of me, far outdoing my lovers who didn't have vulvas. I felt like I orgasmed in 'unwomanly' places such as by masturbating, or rubbing my thighs together, or otherwise anywhere outside of the marital bed – in ways that were not motherly, proper, nor of interest to men. What Deleuze and Guattari point to is a spaciousness within us to overcome what harms us, and to switch up who we are, switch up our gender and our sexuality and all kinds of things that we have been led to believe, by society, are immovable.

As Barker and Iantaffi write, the gender binary is even more deeply rooted in white Western dominant culture than the sexuality binary, with the non-binary nature of gender being even less publicly accepted than the non-binary nature of sexuality.[47] As I write the word 'man' or the word 'woman', I am conscious that I fall into the habits produced by this binary. That is not to say that it is not OK to identify as a man and/or a woman. The point is rather that pain is caused by the need to do so but also due to the idea that gender (and sex) must be fixed, and that one cannot experience gender outside of the binary. The gender binary is also that which is responsible for the requirement that each gender enacts historically, geographically, culturally and socially determined norms, and biological markers of the bodies are also read through these norms.[48] Add to this, that other identities/experiences must be added to experiences of gender, such as indigeneity, race, ethnicity, disability, sexuality, class, age, citizenship, religion or spirituality.[49] Each of these will mean experiences are different, and the stories of Mistresses (or indeed the absence of these stories) show us the interest that society has in silencing the pain experienced. Reading, seeing, understanding and sitting with stories and experiences of gender and sexuality, especially those from people who are different to us, particularly those we are taught to fear, and taught to exclude, because they threaten deeply held (and deeply harmful) belief systems, is a radical act. It is an act of sexual kindness.

Queer pregnant Mistresses

You will remember from the previous chapter that I talked about motherhood and Mistresses, and how being a mother and being a Mistress is something thought to be incompatible. Also thought to be mutually exclusive is being a mother, and not being a woman. Yet we know from Maggie Nelson, that the question as to whether pregnancy is inherently queer is an important one. In *The Argonauts*, she questions how an experience so 'strange and wild and transformative' be regarded as the 'ultimate conformity'.[50] She also asks whether perhaps it is because pregnancy is so tied to femininity that it cannot be radical. Perhaps it is this. Perhaps, since we consider a Mistress to be radical and threatening, and therefore removed from her femininity, we cannot countenance her motherhood. Perhaps too, it is not so binary as this. Perhaps she challenges something deep within the flesh of our assumptions, where the things we have not evolved beyond, such as the gender binary, sexuality binary and white supremacy, take root. It is unthinkable to us that conception, pregnancy and motherhood can and do happen outside of binaries. Queers can fertilize one another. When we hold this truth before us, it becomes a prism through which to observe the pain and possibility of pregnancy unshackled by the sexuality binary.[51] Holding on to the queerness of pregnancy, and conception, and all that comes with it, all the trauma, all the possibility, the loss and the gain, the destruction and the re-birth, is a virtue of sexual kindness.

Time for bed

In the next chapter, we will be looking closely at the sex the Mistress has (inside and outside of the bedroom) and what lessons we might want to learn from it in building a sexually kinder sexuality. In preparation, I want to examine the extent to which the Mistress' pain takes place within the bedroom, and how far this pain extends beyond the act of sex. When we think Mistress, we often think sex, but this is not where the story ends. Strangely, when we think Mistress, we often think 'good' sex, and it is this we might be persuaded to hear about. But as always, there is another story and another kind of sex. It gets messy, as a Mistress.

- When his wife found out about her, she followed her. He left her for his Mistress immediately, of course. This was his wife's signal to replace his obsessions with hers. She crops up in the corner of her vision like a spider executing a surprise drop along its silken thread from a branch above her head. She's never quite sure if she's seen her.

- Sometimes, when he arrives for an afternoon fuck, he smells of her. Not his genitals, well perhaps his genitals, but all of him. His skin smells of them, of their bedroom, of their sofa, of their kitchen, of their dust and debris, of their life, their family, their world. Every breath of him is a breath of her, and a breath of what she does not have.

- There was this one time that they were staying together for a week. He had managed a lie convincing enough to get away for this amount of time, which was usually not possible. Every time she does something domestic, like buying groceries together, like cleaning/clearing the flat they stay in, cooking and especially washing, she feels like she trespasses. This type of everyday stuff, although it makes her heart jump for joy, is not her area. It's not meant for her. She should stick to the bedroom.

- She's Mistress to several people. She feels lucky. She has the life she wants, and all the time in the world, to herself. She's not jealous of them, at least not so much that she can't manage it. She doesn't want to be anyone's anything, let alone wife. She can breathe.

- She's buying her groceries, alone. She sees them. She sees him, his wife and their two children. They look *perfectly happy*, not miserable, like he said.

- Her website analytics show her that there has been a new 'unique visitor' to her website. She can see the search terms used, and they are ones that a new person, unfamiliar with her, would use. The search took place in the village in which her married lover lives with his wife. It must be her.

- He abused her for the length of their relationship. It was amazing at the start, when they didn't see each other so often. It started slowly, and before she knew it, he was under her

skin and his messages made her feel not a rush of love but of
fear. During that time, he told her things that made it clear
that he was abusing his wife, as well as her. He told her a story
that sounded like a rape story. He made it sound like she had
unjustly withheld herself from him. She's free of him now, but
she suspects his wife is not.

- It was her first time having sex with more than one person at
a time. Her partner has been pressuring her for three years
to try 'swinging' or sex with another couple. She initially
liked the idea, but then their sex life became all about seeking
that one thing. Over the years, naturally, she came to think
she could never be enough on her own. They had no open
communication line about how to deal with jealousy and
feeling unsafe – this was shut down by him as 'negativity'.
They met the man in the couple at a sex club, where she had
pleasure-less sex with him and her partner. He had emailed
her partner, asking if they would like to join a small private
'party' of four (compiled of him and his Mistress, and her and
her partner). There was a moment when they were all on the
bed, but it was just her and his Mistress kissing and touching
one another. She made her feel like she was on a peaceful
island, even though she was in the midst of a tumultuous
sea. Her partner tried to intervene in the kiss between the
two women. The Mistress gently pushed him away. She could
not fathom this act of kindness from this Mistress. In the
cab home, her partner described her as 'cock-shy'. Was it an
insult?

- There's a pandemic. The virus is spread through touch and through breath. The government bans everyone from seeing people outside of their household. He cannot, and does not, see her, or any of his other Mistresses, for three months. If he sees any of them, touches any of them, he puts them all at risk, and in ways secret to all of them.

- She wants a baby with him. His wife is pregnant. They've been trying (fucking regularly) for a while.

- When his wife, Marilyn, found out about her, she followed her. He left his Mistress immediately, of course. This was her signal to replace his obsessions with hers. She asks our Mistress to meet with her. Our Mistress is scared. It could be a disastrous meeting. This is what her experience tells her. Upon opening the message, one of her cheeks glows red; it's a sensation like a scar, from when she was slapped in the face before. Little does our Mistress know that, thankfully, his wife was once a Mistress, too.

Story Part IV: How was it for you?

The sex. Is GOOD. One time, we did it on Hampstead Heath. It was well romantic, 'cos around us were cruising men, cruising each other, and those were the sounds I heard, of them making secret steps, as I bent down to grab my ankles while you fucked me. Near my feet, I saw some condom wrappers strewn around, and a copy of *Grazia* with Angelina Jolie on the front. It was exciting, and fun, to, like, see the world. It was *like* that time, when we'd had this row, or more like you just had a go while I cried and waited for you to stop. It took long, but then you fucked me over the bath. It was like that time, when I had four orgasms in a row, in that shit hotel. Then you made me cry again, before going home. Sometimes I think of you fucking her, to make me come. It works. Now your fucking her is not your private thing; it's public in a way – it turns me on, so you can't have it for yourself, like you thought. You can't have secrets from us both. Though you try. Sweaty sex in the pub toilets, which will now fill your dreams, just like I filled you, as you make your journey home to your husband. There was *that* time in that posh hotel in Bloomsbury. When I was on. My period was heavy. I was too shy to tell you because I thought the sex needed to be clean, perfumed and upon pure white sheets for you to want me. That's what I was told anyways. There was a lot of blood. You said you liked it. I was really embarrassed. We've had a lot of sex in woodlands, haven't we? Always among the trees for secret sex. Or dunes for secret public sex, where people can see us. Or roads behind woods, where cars park side by side like pills. Between them are looks, invitations; you want other men to fuck me. By a tree. But not your wife. Let her hand touch me, not yours, for a change. Lead me not to the woods but to your bed; show me what it feels like to stay, and have your morning coffee brought to you by a woman. Let her *fuck* me. Let me feel her tongue in my mouth, in a way that does not take up all the space, like yours. Give me room to speak. Give me sex not in a woodland but in a marital bed, which now becomes a Mistress bed. Tell us, what's the difference?

4

Grimy hotels and dungeons to satin pillows: What's the sex like?

Where, how, when and why do you want me?

The sex can be extraordinary. As a Mistress, it can be momentous. It can be horrendous. Amber Hollibaugh captures this drama perfectly: 'Before there is thought there is sensation and desire... Sex has always been this way for me. Explosive sex I mean – sex that is momentous enough or relentless enough to suck me totally into its it's savage, beautiful whirlpool. That kind of sex – and my craving for it – has configured and reconfigured my life.'[1] This kind of world-making, world-destroying sex is strange, and it makes you strange. It made me strange. Every time I went to meet a married lover, it was like I literally stepped out into another world, as another person. You avoid people, as if traces of being a Mistress are visible in your face, in the way you hold yourself – they probably are. One of the most accurate descriptions of the perfect strangeness of being a Mistress I have read is by James Baldwin, writing in his poem *Munich, Winter 1973*. Baldwin writes of a strangeness that I feel characterizes the Mistress's wait for her lover, the bed upon which she sits, even the whole town in which she walks alone. A delicious strangeness descends and, as Baldwin writes, surrounds a 'very strange me' who 'is waiting for you'.[2]

As much as being a Mistress can cause our bodies to morph strangely in time with hotel rooms, and be caught in a glorious romance, being a Mistress can also be destructive, unwanted and traumatic. But perhaps to think of sex this way, particularly as something inherent to the experience of being a Mistress doesn't help us, when trying to change how we think of the Mistress's place in our societies. We think Mistress: we think constant champagne, dangerous liaisons, satin, roses, tears, drama, being caught and being destroyed/destructive, wanton, thoughtless. Yes, it is the sex that creates new worlds, but only bad ones. We think of Mistress sex as always being extraordinary, but somehow empty. But what if we could learn something from Mistress's experiences of sex? What if there is something about the sex she has, and the restrictions placed upon it, such as space and time; such as being 'lovers against the wind' that could teach us something surprising about how to get the sex we want, that nourishes us, and to recognize and reject the sex we don't? I have had extraordinary Mistress sex in hotel rooms where I have felt restored, loved, held, empowered and safe; I have also had extraordinary Mistress sex in hotel rooms where I have felt depleted as I circulate the tumultuous whirlpool, less than who I was before, lonely, disempowered and unsafe. Where are the differences and what can they tell us – do we really want the sex the Mistress has?

In her Biomythography, *Zami: A New Spelling of My Name*, Audre Lorde expresses a feeling of being at sea among desire, knowing that with want, can come a lack of safety: 'I knew what I wanted, which was everybody at one time, and since my wants felt contradictory, I had to figure out some way I could have everything that I wanted and still be safe. That was very difficult, because we were in unchartered territory.'[3] The Mistress is always in contradiction, since her wants are never what she *should* want. As such, she is never safe. When it is a matter of who a Mistress desires, who a woman desires, who a Black woman desires and particularly when the object of desire (directly, or indirectly) is another woman, territory is always unknown. There is no road map, because we didn't know there was a road. There is no story. The Mistress resides in no man's land, and by extension has never been allowed her own path. Each step she takes as she follows her desire will be risky and uncertain. Unlike permitted relationships, even radical relationships such as polyamory, there is no road map to how sex, particularly ethical sex, should look to a Mistress. If we're not able to talk about it, then of course the where, how, when and why of sex as a Mistress are unknown and, as such, always risky (and/or exciting, depending on what turns you on).

Where: hotel dreaming

Some will say that this lack of safety is sexy. It's risky, it's exciting, – that's what makes a Mistress, and sex with her, desirable. I want to urgently challenge this idea. The Mistress might seem like she lives a dream, but it is important to recognize that she does not exist only there, in our fantasies, but also as flesh and blood. In Octavia Butler's short story, 'The Book of Martha', in the volume *Bloodchild*, the protagonist, a poor Black woman, is given the responsibility by god to save humanity from itself, at which point she must return to live among them as one the 'lowliest'.[4] Martha's solution, through conversation with god, is to create a world where humans have an ethics-free, boundless, hyper-real environment to live out their pleasures: their dreams. These dreams would be much more intense than usual dreams, so that the dreamers would be satisfied; yet they would also retain their self-respect and their duties to their families. As Martha decides, and Butler writes in her afterword, utopias are only possible in dreams. But even then, it seems that we must wake up. And wake up we must. It is as though Book of Martha has been written for the Mistress, since it is she who often inhabits the dream in a world without ethics, so that normal, responsible-seeming married life can continue. This is precisely where it is safe (for) us to keep the Mistress, but she does not experience this world as a pain-free utopia, and it is far from ethics-free.

Hotels sell us these kinds of dreams. They sell us a room of our own, with crisp sheets: a place to play, away from all the bad things that happen, a refuge, a holiday from time and normality. They well us secrecy in a space that has facilitated intimacy for a thousand other stories before yours, but shows no evidence of them. Where do these stories go? I have cried my most painful and bitter tears in a hotel room, as the door slides shut, at the hands of a man who thinks he is living out his dream. Where do those tears go? For the Mistress, the hotel room is likely to be her strange home. It will probably be paid for with a corporate business card, or perhaps with cash. It will likely be, and certainly has been in my experience, that the Mistress will meet her lover at between 2 and 4 pm, when check-in is allowed. She might meet her lover in the hotel bar, or more likely, in the room itself, where she might spend time making it nice: softening the lighting, drawing the curtains, removing the polyester bed runner. Her lover will then arrive. Sex feels compulsory in these rooms, in these settings: it is as though nothing else is possible. To be fair, what else is there to do, other than watch the huge television, and/or order overpriced food and drink from room service?

When we see Mistresses in films, the hotel room always makes an appearance. Seeing Ronit meet Esti (who is an orthodox Jewish woman, married to Dovid), for their illicit and incredibly dangerous liaison in the film adaptation of *Disobedience*, given what is at stake, you could easily think the London hotel room is on the side of the Mistress. It is not a complicated room – business-like, with mass-produced light, pine-coloured flat pack units and doors that slip shut in a neat and functional way. The sex they have is hot. There is a light, playful and erotic feel to their fucking and the drab room just looks on, as if to say, 'Yes I let this happen, aren't I grand?' In this sense, the role of the hotel room in *Disobedience* is not unusual. The figure of the hotel will be familiar to anyone who has been or is a Mistress, and those who have watched any kind of film which features a Mistress since cinema began, and read any kind of book in which there is an affair. It is as if this is where she lives. It is as though this is her home, and where she is allowed intimacy: the hotel room is necessary to her sexuality. It is as though we cannot, or don't want to, think of her as an inhabitant in her own home. Perhaps it is because we want to keep her out of *our* home.

Where: else?

The sex in hotel rooms can be *incredible*. But so can sex in the bedroom, dogging and in dungeons, in sex clubs, in toilets and in back streets. What strikes me about the best sex I've had is that its quality has depended on the safety I have felt, even though the setting might be associated with danger and risk. As a Mistress, sex in dangerous settings (whether the danger comes from the likelihood of being caught or harmed physically, psychologically or emotionally) is just necessary given the undisclosed nature of the relationship(s) she has. She needs to be out of sight. She must be away from the eyes of her lover's spouse/partner(s), perhaps friends too, family, and those who will judge her. Her lover requires this of her too, whether or not she wishes it to be this way. Perhaps she would like to have sex in the open and be discovered, and to change this story, once and for all. Perhaps not, perhaps she loves the secrecy, or needs the secrecy for her own safety. Whatever the qualities of a particular Mistress's story, the space in which she has sex takes on a particular danger, as well as magic, since it is secret, mysterious and, to the world, a space where too many lines are crossed.

In Smart's *Grand Central Station*, there is a constant sense of crossing boundaries, even when Smart is doing things that are considered completely normal and usually trouble-free for someone who is not a Mistress. Yet every space, not only the spaces in which she has sex, causes her to feel vulnerable, as if she wears her sins, and as if she looks *strange*. It will not matter where she goes in this world, because it is not made for her. It is not made for her, because space is made for families – white, heterosexual, cis-gendered families.

The world depends upon it, and guards its territory fiercely and jealously. As Lynda Johnston and Robyn Longhurst argue in *Space, Place and Sex*, there is a theoretical idea that private space tends to be for women, and public space is for men to dominate. This idea flows from the position that women are more at home (at home); and men go out to work, and inhabit and control public space. Women stay out of public space because it is dangerous, and because, why would they need to be there, if they have a home? Acceptable ways of having sex and acceptable people with whom to have sex are also dictated by this model. Space is a way of keeping us, our genders and our sexual identities and experiences safe, and therefore, in line.[5]

Researchers throughout the decades have found Foucault's position to be true: that space is a way to control sexuality, even when we think we are transgressing out of sight.[6] Even sexual practices that we might think inherently strange or dangerous, such as cruising/cottaging, swinging and public sex, become controlled since they tend to happen in spaces that are recognizable, and therefore contained. The case of the Mistress is interesting since the sex she has falls into the 'deviant' category yet it might not necessarily appear so. She may just be having what we might call 'vanilla' sex, in permitted spaces such a hotel, or perhaps in a lover's bedroom, or her own. Or could be having sex in a deviant space, because that is the only space available to her and her lover.

What freaks us out is that she crosses the line without us knowing, and that by crossing this sacred line, she violates something that we feel ownership over. We are not even sure why, but she deserves whatever punishment she gets. She crosses without even moving – just by *being*. Her silent rebellion, that she cannot (or must not) reveal (because we punish her if she does) and her sexual kindness that we dare not name, or allow ourselves to see, is what we fear. As bell hooks writes, we often fear because we fear radical change, and as such, we betray our hearts and minds. If only we were able to love, then fear would necessarily leave.[7] The Mistress is telling us that *something* about how we are approaching relationships, sex and love, is nonsense. She is calling us out. She is asking us to wake up, but we want to stay asleep, escaping our fears through our ethics-free world of dreams. The Mistress is reminding us that it is possible to love, and be kind, if we could just push through the fear. Who knows what could be waiting for us. A Mistress is both a casualty of the lines she crosses in secret and a pioneer, since she crosses the threshold nonetheless.

How?

bell hooks writes that it is no accident that we are scared, and it is no accident that we think that love is only love if it is edgy, unknown and mysterious, or that we do not think that love and kindness can be present together.[8] The image of the Mistress as dangerous and mysterious, and that her home, in your mind (and mine), is the cheap hotel room, is because those in power, through media, moral and political representations, have told us so. It is also true that the Mistress has hardly been given a chance to provide an alternative to this story. Perhaps if we listen to our Mistresses, we might be able to learn how sexual kindness makes for good sex. Then we might be able to circumvent the fear that prevents us from loving our Mistress in the way she deserves.

So, let's get down to it! Here are seven short scenarios based on sex I have had as a Mistress, and I'd like you to pay close attention to what it is about my identity as Mistress, or any identities present in the encounter, that affects the quality and feel of the sex, and whether this quality caused me to experience harm or pleasure. A note of caution here: there are some aspects within these stories that are difficult to read since they include sexual assault. Sexual assault and rape are never the fault of the survivor, whether or not they are a Mistress.[9]

1. It is a hotel room, again. We do as we always do, which is undress one another immediately once we have entered the room. He's on his knees for a while, licking my clit. It feels OK. I feel a little powerful. I feel delicious excitement in my stomach, that we will have sex, followed by food. I feel a compulsion to do well at being a Mistress. Then he fucks me. It feels good, and I come. Something is sneaking into body – it's a lot like dread. I push it away. I make him come by sucking his cock and slowly edging two fingers up inside him, which I know he loves. I am a professional, after all. He comes. The dread is now taking root fully, as he holds me in his afterglow. I am ahead of the game, though. When he begins talking, I know that I need to shape my answers in a way that won't upset him. I also need to talk for as long as I can, so he has less time to bring the conversation to my sexual past and my 'untrustworthiness'. I want to make it through one time, where this doesn't happen. Then we will be making progress. I never succeed. He washes his cock in the shower, before he leaves, presumably in case she goes there after me. He doesn't try to hide it.

2. This time we can't stay in a hotel, since he needs to be at home
   first thing in the morning. I don't ask why; I don't want to
   know. We are together now. We have a drink in our favourite
   pub and we kiss, like teenagers, in a secret corner. We go for a
   walk and we enter one of those beautiful old (usually locked)
   squares that can surprise you as you walk around London.
   We sit on a bench, and I am wet. We are kissing a lot, and I
   am feeling his erection through his trousers and it feels so
   hard, so eager, so fearless – I want to suck it but I can't; we
   can't because people could appear from anywhere. He finger
   fucks me. He doesn't come and it doesn't matter. It doesn't
   feel incomplete; it feels joyful. We feel like there is no one
   else in this world, and it is just us, against the wind, against
   everything. I am happy *because* I am his Mistress.

3. We are walking on Hampstead Heath. It is a place for cruising,
   usually for queer men; but we are queer women, so it's all the
   same, right? I am not used to being in charge, or feeling like
   I am allowed a say in what happens. We walk and walk, and
   I am confused because usually by now, the sex would have
   happened. I am her Mistress, but I feel an unfamiliar sense
   of control and choice. Against a tree, she kisses me. I am
   focused on my need to see and touch her breasts, and to feel
   her lips on my clit. Seeing her kneeling on the ground, among
   the debris of used lube sachets, knowing someone could see
   me, with this woman on her knees sucking me, thrills me.
   It's good sex. Afterwards, I don't think I feel shame, but I feel
   sad. Because I know once she is gone, she is gone. She never

returns my calls, emails, messages – not until she wants to see me and fuck some more.

4. I don't feel like I am his Mistress, but I am. We meet as often as we can, and when we do, he never leaves the hotel at 6 pm. He always stays the night. He loves my freedom, and he loves himself. He respects me, but explores and excites me. One thing I love about being a Mistress is how I feel like a Goddess, like the one who gives him everything he needs and misses. It is true I feel like this, but I know that the sex we have is not filling a void in his soul. We are in a hotel room. The room is not so different from the hotel rooms I have stayed in before as a Mistress – anonymous, plush, full of white cotton. We fuck on the bed and the sex is remarkably similar in movement, position and character to what I have had before with husbands. Except, we bathe in one another's smells of all kinds, drink them in and take refuge in clouds of them. It is delicious and homely fucking. The orgasm is more intense, and I am not ashamed after. I am not scared about what will happen now he has come. I am a Mistress in love, and he doesn't doubt it.

5. I have been in sex/swingers' clubs many times. On the internet forums, people say that they love these places since there is none of that 'cheating' business; 'I just have sex with my Mistresses right in front of my wife!' They make it sounds like some post-monogamy utopia, like Martha's world; it is free of your usual ethics and you can live out your adulterous dreams. It is not so. Or rather, it can be so, but it is not so much of a dream for everyone.

6. I have three men in mind, to whom I was a Mistress. All
    of them abused me, in different ways, but they share one
    common thing, aside from being my abusers: they all raped
    me. They all thought they were fantastic, romantic and sensual
    lovers. As a Mistress, I never questioned it – I assumed I
    deserved it and that it was my fault for being in the wrong in
    the first place. I now know this is not so, and never so.

Sexy safety

Contrary to what is popular belief, a Mistress has better sex the safer
she feels. It is tempting to imagine that her greatest pleasures are had
when she is in the most dangerous, risky, exciting and titillating (for
us) scenarios. However, this is more about the fantasies that we have,
and the ones that we have been told to have, than about the reality of
having and experiencing sexuality, as a Mistress. Simply put, safety
does not equal sexy in how we imagine exciting sex as a Mistress.

Speaking from my own experience, excitement and risk can equal
sexy. But it can also not. Likewise, safety, mundanity and anything
vanilla-flavoured can be very sexy, and sometimes not. It is a very
difficult balance to strike, given the time and space restrictions that
usually contain Mistress relationships. So, what are the key ingredients
and key lessons we can learn? Lesson one (and ingredient one) is
sexy safety. Sexy safety is safety, but naughtier and more ethical. The
foundation of sexy safety is that the Mistress asks us to be sexually
kind, and therefore honest, that Mistress sex is, paradoxically, never
safe for the Mistress.

As bell hooks reminds us, 'The practice of love offers no place of safety. We risk loss, hurt, pain. We risk being acted upon by forces outside our control.'[10] She also writes, 'Too often women, and some men, have their most intense erotic pleasure with partners who wound them in other ways... The best sex and the most satisfying sex are not the same.'[11] Here, we find the perfect framing for sexy safety. First, we need to remember that with love, particularly 'outsider love', comes the possibility of pain. The Mistress opens herself to this danger as the 'other woman'. Remember, as we know from the previous chapter, a Mistress is (at least) doubly othered, as both woman and outsider and threat to our deeply held and treasured institution of sacred straight love. Yes, she takes her particular chance, but she opens herself to all the general risks that come with loving, *and then some*. For this, she needs, but does not get, our respect, comfort nor communication. Second, there is a pronounced difference between great and satisfying (or what I have called 'nourishing') sex. This is a difference that the Mistress will know more than most for reasons I will talk about, but include the time and circumstances for reflection (think: Anaïs Nin), and the physical, psychological and emotional risk (as well as unique possibilities for pleasure) that she is exposed to every time she has sex.

Once again, I find myself deferring to the kink community for the importance of safety in sex, particularly regarding sex which places the participant outside of what is conventionally accepted sexual expression. As we know from the previous chapter, open commination surrounding both wanted and unwanted aspects of a sexual encounter is common to ethical BDSM encounters. This acknowledges the exposure to physical, emotional and psychological risk that sex generally brings. Yes, BDSM can be more dangerous because of the kind of acts it involves. But that is exactly the point: BDSM practitioners know that because of their particular sexual practice, and by virtue of being outsiders, they know that sex can render us both powerful and vulnerable, and that, whether we want it to or not, sex takes place within power dynamics. So, why can we not treat sex with Mistresses in the same way? Can we not acknowledge the uniqueness of the risks, the particular (often multiple) harms to which she is exposed as a Mistress? Can we not allow her to have her Herethics? Sometimes, the emotional risk will be more than the physical, or the psychological, depending on who she is, and who her lover is, but they will always be greater because of how deeply outside of our ethical consciousness she is. Sometimes she will also be additionally marginalized due to her race, gender identity, class, sexuality or disability. Because we think of Mistresses as Herethical, we think of Mistresses as incapable of being harmed in the same sense of, say, a wife, or 'good', 'moral', person could be. Yet a Mistress's experience of sex is volatile and fragile. The experience can easily cross over from being pleasurable to traumatic, from exciting danger to dangerous excitement, from romance to pain, from fear to adventure.

Practising sexy safety

So what does the practice of sexy safety look like? Let's take Scenes 1 and 4 from the list above. They take place in the same kind of space, which is a chain hotel room. They also take place with different people, but every person is de facto different, and every experience is different. The 'that was just one bad man/husband/person' is a common argument designed to invalidate stories of intimate patriarchal violence – the familiar *not all men* argument. It is, of course, designed to protect the power that keeps Mistresses. Both scenes take place between me and a married white cis man who is significantly older than me, and in a position of greater power than me. In both scenes I am a graduate student, and they are both professors. In both scenes I feel a power from being an outsider, and a sexual rush from the effect I am having on the men I am fucking. In both scenes, the fucking is exciting, passionate and romantic, carrying all the hallmarks of Mistress sex.

If you have read some of the erotic works of Anaïs Nin, such as *Eros Unbound*,[12] *Henry and June* and *A Spy in the House of Love*, then you will be even more easily able to detect the crucial difference between these two scenes. In reading Nin, you can feel the power in her voice, the lack of judgement, whether she tells the story through first- or third-person narration. You feel safe to touch yourself while you read her – in fact, you are expected to. There is a similar quality to Nicholson Baker's *Vox* and his later work, *House of Holes*. The women who are part of the encounters feel able to say what they want and are never made to feel bad for doing so. Only good and pleasurable things happen when they do. Some of the scenes are bizarre in these books – such as penis washing, fucking a headless man-bot or a penis tree, a perverse tattooist, a seductive disembodied arm, straw portals, 'plasmic genitals', fucked-with language such as 'dicktitude', 'loin stem' and 'testosterdick' and an unapologetic celebration of orgasms, clitorises, bodies and fluid sexuality.[13] It just feels right. And here lies the difference between Scenes 1 and 4. In Scene 1, I held the power because of the sex, yet when it finished, not only did I lose what I had, I ricocheted back to below zero: back to Mistress in pain.

In Scene 4, my power existed before the sex. Yes, I was a Mistress, but I was not treated differently because I was. My needs were not neglected, and not only did I enjoy the pleasure in Scene 4, there was an open line of communication around the more difficult aspects. There was an overwhelming sense of safety among the risk, and that meant freedom in pleasure. Of course, there were still difficulties, but the crucial element in Scene 4 that made the sex nourishing was not about the space, nor necessarily the time (though it helps, for me at least, when a lover stays the night), not even that my lover was kind, but because our relationship and the sex was, despite being unethical, entirely ethical in the sense that we were invested in making one another stronger, not weaker. We had a Mistress Ethic, built on the virtues of sexual kindness. One of those virtues is nourishing sex.

The fluid mundane

Due to time and space constraints, as a Mistress it is possible to gain an extraordinary appreciation of the mundanity of relationships – you find a certain glee in bodily fluids, and an extraordinary and erotic joy in activities like watching TV together. It is not because you are grateful for the crumbs of a life of which you are jealous that belongs to their wife but because you have the opportunity, as a Mistress, to observe, feel, see, bask and reflect upon these things – to indulge in them, like in some kind of joyful erotic sex lab. The gift of Mistress-hood is the ability to see, and find, more magic than most. This is not a gift I feel I would have had, had I not been a Mistress for so long and so often. I am not a Mistress now, but I still have and love this gift. As much as Mistress-hood can be a container for pain, it can be a container for intimacy. It is as though being a Mistress encourages understanding about what you want, since the circumstances make it so abundantly clear what is nourishing and what is not. It is also a fantastic arsehole filter: those who treat their Mistress badly are, after all, of a certain kind, and best avoided.

Sex fluids are an effective focalizer for understanding this curious gift that a Mistress acquires. The Mistress understands that sex fluids are of great consequence in bringing both damage and joy. Let's look again at Scene 1 and what my lover does before he leaves me in the hotel room. That he does it will likely not shock you, since it seems sensible, right? If she fucks him after me, she will smell something different to what she expects, and become suspicious. The same lover tells me how much he loves the smell of my cunt on him. I also love all his smells, from semen to the remnants of butt smell on my finger. There is a sensation that can come with fluid, too, fluid that you cannot wash off, that remains inside you. You do not have the privilege of hiding, or escaping it by showering, but you do get a different 'gift'. Charlotte Roche's narrator in *Wetlands* speaks of fluids in exactly this way: they are a gift to her, because not only do they smell and feel good (like when sperm seeps out of your vagina, if you have one) but because they are really, really, naughty.[14] They are a gift to a sexual revolutionary like a Mistress. This is so because to talk about them (or not) has massive implications. If you talk about them, you could be seen as dirty, impolite, slutty, inappropriate; yet if you don't, you are repressed, and also complicit in society's silence around (particularly women's) bodies and sexuality. If you talk about them, especially to a particular person/people (or you don't), as a Mistress, things happen.

The things that happen can be big, such as not only complicit in society's silence but your lover's. If you do talk about them, you could cause big changes, the end of marriages, perhaps. It's not fair though, of course, since the responsibility to not talk falls on you. You can't win, when it comes to spunk.

And yet, you do. As a Mistress, your fluids are powerful, because they can change the world, or people's worlds. If yours are found, felt or smelt – that's the end of a world, someone's world, perhaps multiple worlds. It could also be the beginning, or the much needed break in a silence. As a Mistress, you also get to develop an appreciation of whatever your chosen sticky bodily poison might be – pussy juice, perhaps. You know how developing a taste for it, for the body's fruits, can be the pleasurable gift that keeps on giving.

Kindness, queer romance and revolution

Maggie Nelson reminds us that there is something inescapably sexy about realizing the revolutionary capacity of bodies. She writes, while in her feminist theory class, '[labial lips] make a circle that is always self-touching, an autoerotic mandorla... It reminded me that a lot of women can jerk off just by pressing their legs together on a bus or a chair or whatever.'[15] Concepts that promise revolution, or empower our bodies sexually, are sexy, and I agree with Nelson – it is *very* easy to get juiced up.

Speaking of this, let's return to Scenes 3 and 5 above. From Chapter 3, we know that bisexuality is always somehow a part of Mistress relationships, and a part of Mistresses. This is part of their revolutionary power. We also know that bisexuality and Mistress-hood have something in common: they can be spaces (both literal and within ourselves) that take us away from our lives, or they can be people, who take us away from ourselves. Cixous writes about this infinite possibility in *The Book of Promethea*. Here we find Cixous's attempt at describing love between women, both specifically (for a particular woman) and abstractly (for women generally): 'She will always be there. But she is not always where she is. She is not far away but often I don't know where she is, in what city, what she is turning into and what shape she is taking. She is always in transfiguration.'[16] I found her on Hampstead Heath, and I found her in the sex club. What we learn is that she cannot be idealized, since she can still treat a Mistress badly. It is not about the gender of an encounter, or even its sexuality; it's about whether sexual kindness is present. A condition of this sexual kindness is that the encounter brings about a nourishing, sexy safe, space for the Mistress. This space must be for the Mistress, as a Mistress, and must not make her wish she wasn't, but joyous that she is.

Daddy who?

I have previously dismissed the idea of the one 'bad' man being the variable that can cause an experience to change from nourishing to harmful. That we would attribute so much power to one man to change the entire character of experience, given what we know about the complex personal, bodily, political, social and legal elements that compile our sexual encounters, is telling. This is part of why we don't want to talk about Mistress sex: we don't want to upset this man, that lives on in our hearts and minds – the man of that says: down girl, and coincidently (or not), the man who often keeps a Mistress. I would like to remind the reader that there might be those, people of all genders, who might hold a Mistress, but not keep and own a Mistress, and this man would, and does. This is the man in Scene 1, and all the men in Scene 6. Consensually non-monogamous men (and women), who are aware of their power, can be glorious, and the Mistress ought never be ashamed to love him, just as he ought not be ashamed to love her.

One of the oft-cited defences of husbands who have Mistresses, and often the ones who have treated their Mistresses badly – one advanced by themselves and by their wives, is that they are a 'family man', as if this places them beyond reproach. The implication is that they are so upstanding, and therefore it is unlikely that they would have a Mistress, or if they did/do, then it is because that dirty Jolene made him do it. As uncomfortable as it may seem, fathers can have Mistresses, as well as daughters. And sometimes, those Mistresses are the same age as their daughters.

Katherine Angel reminds us in *Daddy Issues* that 'feminism and fathers have long been entangled, often in antagonism'.[17] While men tend to easily be seen as the perpetrators of sexual violence, the said perpetrator tends to be any man, any man but my dad.[18] Yet, I can tell you that I have been a Mistress to five men who were fathers as well as husbands. There are also many famous (historical and contemporary) powerful men who have or had Mistresses while being fathers, along with many non-famous ones. A hands-on father is, as Angel writes, often lauded as a hero (whereas the mother is simply a mother).[19] The fathers I was Mistress to (who also, incidentally, were the most abusive of lovers) tended to pride themselves on how involved they were with their children, and how much they loved them. What I have also observed is the cringeworthy 'personal over-investment' in their daughter's sex lives and partner choices;[20] yet they have no concern for their Mistress's sexual well-being. Yet it is true, though, that there is often the same jealously and possessiveness. A father's treatment of his daughter and that of his Mistress are both the same and different, in the worst possible ways. In short, as Angel tells us, fathers must remain on the hook generally,[21] but also specifically here, for understanding their complicity in a lack of ethics for the Mistress.

Ironically, the Mistress (particularly if her partners are older than her) will often be the one who is framed as having 'daddy issues'. She will be the one, like me, like Hollibaugh, like many Mistresses, who is accused of having daddy issues, a euphemism for having been abused in her past – she is harmfully portrayed as irrevocably damaged yet always a 'good time'. It is important to question as to why the mental health status of a Mistress causes us, as a society, or as a partner, to treat her worse, or consider her less entitled to ethical treatment. We also know, from Chapter 2, that Mistress-hood is likely to be seen as conflicting with motherhood as it is constructed in Western society. Yet having a Mistress does not conflict with ideas around the 'fatherliness' of her lovers. We also know that a married lover is likely to be extra attentive to the idea to *avoiding* becoming a father (where both the Mistress and lover are cis-gendered people having a heterosexual encounter).

bell hooks writes that a relationship that is not founded on 'true' (ethical) love simply replays 'family dramas'.[22] Mistress relationships reveal more than others, about the harms wrought by these irresistible, hidden family dramas. Therefore a crucial part of Mistress ethics is in acknowledging how daddy issues impact women in the absence of Mistress ethics, and how acknowledging them – and how they will also impact different marginalized identities such as race, religion, disability, sexual orientation and gender identity, in greater and more complex ways – can bring us closer to understanding sexual kindness.

When? A haunting

Timing is important as a Mistress. Time is also different to a Mistress. The past takes on different dimensions, as much as the present takes on a different intensity, as much as the future becomes uncertain, or rather, can become painfully certain. He leaves or he doesn't. I want to talk about all three of these familiar linear temporal dimensions and past, present and future, and repopulate them with an understanding of how a Mistress lives them. I begin, as I must, with the present.

Present – The sensuality of the Mistress forces her into the present. She is connected to it in a way that has a specific intensity. The moments she experiences, as we have seen from the stories I have been asking you to read, carry a particular extra-marital weight: she is hyper-aware of her position in society due to how she is being treated in any given moment. This can be a gift and a curse since as much as she is aware of abuse and judgement, she is also hyper-aware of beauty, wonder, romance, profound sexual awareness and connection, love, the joys of intimacy and the magic of the mundane.

Past – The Mistress and the wife haunt one another. The Mistress is always a possibility to marriage, and the wife is always there to the

Mistress, even when she isn't. The Mistress is usually a ghost, since she is secret, impersonal – yet she is vivid in our minds when someone says, 'Mistress'. There are always traces or one of the other, no matter how hard they are scrubbed from a body. Ghosts of lives lived, and to be lived, in secret, hang in the air and grace fantasies. When I moved in with my married lover, after she left, I felt her presence in everything. I needed to purge the place, but the traces remained. I remember being told that I deserved everything I got since she was there first. Perhaps that's why she haunted me so. The Mistress is not only the ghost of a present and specific body but is a haunted body – haunted by judgement. The Mistress identity carries ghostly remainders of Mistresses and Witches burnt at the stake across the ages – she is both timeless and timely.[23] She haunts people and marriages, and remains a threat across time to marriage and the treasured principles, laws and ideas that we consider the fabric of society. The great thing is, though, in being timeless, she is relentless.

Future – The future, for the Mistress, is full of questions that will mean different things depending on the identity of the specific Mistress and her circumstances. Will he leave her? What if he does? What will his children think of me? What if he doesn't? Friends keep asking if he will, while they all marry and get their own Mistresses. Do I want children? Will I get children? Do I want a partner? When will we be able to see one another again? Will he have a crisis of conscience? Will she find out? What will she do? What if everyone finds out? What if they find out? Will I be safe? Will I keep my job? Will I keep my friends? Will I be happy? Am I wrong to want to continue to live this way? Am I wrong to not? What will he do if I leave? What will he do if I don't? Will I ever be enough? Do I want to be the 'other woman'?

How will I handle the loss, the grief and the possibility of the wife's life I am not living? Do I want something else entirely, beyond all the possibilities of even sex-positivity and polyamory? Why can't I imagine it?

The big questions

- Does she really want her lover to leave their husband/wife partner? If she says she doesn't, is she lying (to you and herself)? She probably is lying (after all this is what she's best at).

- She said that she likes being the Mistress. That's why he likes coming to her. It's been that way for years and years. She's lost track of the years, the things she's missed, but she's grown used to it. No one asks her about a plus-one anymore. No one asks her if she'll marry or have children (that's one big advantage, to be honest). They don't talk about it and this works, mostly, as a way of avoiding the pain. They never did talk about it. She's long past the point where she might snap. Their relationship has a beautiful rhythm and, despite the years, is abundant with romance and sexual passion. And yet, there will be a time, a few more years from now, when she *will* snap. She will say to him, 'You chose to believe I was fine. You chose not to talk about it, or let me talk about it' – not with a violence that you can see, but with a power that kept a little part of me waiting and, barely, surviving. Things could be much worse. He's not *that* bad, is he?

- He says he'll leave her. They definitely sometimes leave, these husbands, she read, somewhere on the internet. There was a statistic that said something like 10 per cent eventually leave. How can they *possibly* know this? How can they know how many extra-marital relationships there are, since people are afraid to disclose them? How can they know how many of her there are? In any case, he's bound to be one of the 10 per cent. Just as she is about to close her browser, she sees an article about Mistresses having 'daddy issues' and being 'mate-stealers' who are irrevocably damaged and unworthy. The article is written by a middle-class white woman, who's been through it all and she's so thankful her husband 'saw the light' and knew he would understand that one should never 'marry their Mistress' and remembered how loyal his wife had been. The article ends with 'good men stay away from bad women'. Is she a bad woman?

- The relationship isn't amazing, but after all, she's supposed to want him to leave her, so she can be a whole person in a whole complete relationship. She needs that. Society needs her to need that. She might be happier if he just, well, didn't. If he leaves, her life will be disrupted, and to be honest, she senses something 'off' about him. He suffocates her when things are good, and she's trembling with anxiety, broken when things are bad. This can't be right. She's not jealous of his wife; she's fearful for her. As Offred says in *The Handmaid's Tale*, 'You can only be jealous of someone who has something you think you ought to have yourself.' Should he leave?

- The relationship is amazing, but she doesn't ask him to leave, since it doesn't make much difference if he does. She loves things how they are, and so does he. Is there something wrong?

- Would it just not be much better (and more virtuous and ethical) if everyone just disclosed everything, like all the sex-positive feminists tell us to do? She read this somewhere and so felt ashamed. In fact, because she thinks she will feel a sense of validation and support with the LGBTQ+ and Kink Community, she has been following a lot of influencers and key members of these communities on social media, and reading a lot of sex-positive literature. Sometimes it helps. Some of it's awesome. And then, she realizes, they often don't mean to include her. Disclosure is always both ethical and necessary. She steps back from these communities, and feels a sense of shame. She's the undisclosed. She can be as out as she wants, but part of her will have to remain in the closet, for her own safety. Sex positivity does not (mean to) include Mistresses, does it?

- Would it be better if she didn't leave her wife? So they could keep the romance and the magic. She is her Promethea; she is everything – the sun and the moon, her joy and her pain. She feels the sense that they have, and will meet, in every lifetime. She writes poetry about her. If she leaves, it will all slip away and dissolve. Sometimes, things are meant to be this way, aren't they?

Story Part V: Your life together begins

Finally! He told his wife about you. You've been waiting for this day for months. Today's the day. You talked together, the day before, to make plans about what to do when she chucks him out on the street. He'll come straight to you. *It's happening!* How your heart sings. Your life together can begin. You go to the supermarket and get enough in so that you can make a supper for two. Mountains of fresh fragrant herbs. You've already been looking at houses to rent. It'll be something small for now, since you and he agreed that he'll need to give a lot of his money to his wife and children. But that's OK. As long as we're together, you say. It won't be long and he'll divorce her and he'll be able to remarry ... you've even talked about having your own children.

He said he'll be talking to her about mid-morning, so you should stay by your phone, and expect his call any time after 12, really. He'll then jump on the train straight away and come to you, though it might be late. That's OK, you say; 12 comes and goes. As does 3 pm, 4 pm, 5 pm and even 9 pm. You sleep restlessly and wake early. The call still hasn't come. The call doesn't come, and nor does he.

5

Three's a crowd and more than 'each other': Why is the Mistress wrong?

Those who stay and those who leave

If you are a Mistress reading this, then you might be asking the question: will they leave their partner? It might be because you want them to, or it might be because you don't. If you are a partner knowing your partner has a Mistress, you might be asking the same question for the same reasons. As Audre Lorde wrote in *A Litany for Survival*, 'when we are loved we are afraid love will vanish, when we are alone we are afraid love will never return.'[1] And thus defines our condition, and perpetual clinging to the ubiquitous pillar that holds a mirage of certainty – monogamy. If things remain as they are in terms of our attitudes to the Mistress, then I would suggest that, sadly, we are right to be afraid.

It is impossible to say if he or she will leave, since this is not a topic deemed worthy of sustained and rigorous academic/research enquiry. I have fallen into this trap myself, spending hours scouring the internet for evidence that I am not making a fool of myself by waiting. The more sensible answer would be that a partner leaves their partner when they are ready to, whether or not they have a Mistress. After all the painful paths towards knowing how a Mistress is kept, and how a wife is taken, we are, however, left with this big question. As Bharati Mukherjee writes in her powerfully anti-colonial, time-hopping, trauma-folding tale of a serial Mistress, *Jasmine*, 'The world is divided between those who stay and those who leave.'[2] The narrator, Jasmine, who is from a small village in Punjab, is talking to Karin, the white wife of her white married lover Bud, who leaves Karin for her. For Jasmine, Bud's leaving might be due to a desire for atonement for being American, healthy and in love. And also because of the extravagance of their love. What is for sure, though, is that whether it is atonement, extravagance, fear, safety, redemption of corruption, and whether it is for a wife or a Mistress, something determines whether we stay or go. Perhaps it is courage, or bravery, or perhaps it is falling in love with oneself that determines the fall of the pendulum towards leaving or staying. Neither is easy, particularly for the Mistress. Yet the division is how we determine the worth of a Mistress. If she is a 'good' Mistress, he leaves for her; if she is 'bad', he stays with his wife. Yet from the preceding four chapters, we know that a Mistress is worth everything. She is always worth leaving for. So there is a better, kinder, question to ask: why would she want him to leave?

This is the bit that bothers us. Deep in our unconscious mind, in the architecture of our ego, in the vows we give to our heart, in the claim we lay over our lover's bodies, is the notion that husband and wife belong together, to the exclusion of all others. The world promised us this, that we could own another. This is why the Mistress enflames us all. She reveals the nonsense that is this promise. Regimes of ethical non-monogamy and polyamory give the impression of offering us, the Mistress, and those who have Mistresses a more ethical path, yet it is a path not often followed by either party. There have long been Mistresses, there are Mistresses and there will always be Mistresses, but why, when these alternatives are available? And given what we now know from the four chapters leading us here, how can we, with this knowledge, make her future kinder?

Polyamory versus monogamy

In *Written on the Body*, Winterson cuts right to the heart of it: 'How can you say that to one person and gladly fuck another? Shouldn't you take that vow and break it the way you made it, in the open air? Odd that marriage, a public display and free to all, gives way to that most secret of liaisons, an adulterous affair.'[3] This is the enduring paradox that polyamory hopes to overcome, that indeed fucking another should not vitiate your vow to committed partners. However, despite the juicy adversarial promise of this section heading, I will not be pitting both perfectly legitimate relationship structures against one another, nor measuring either's success. Rather, I will be looking at what values we can find within each, and whether they help or harm the Mistress. I cannot consider the Mistress as within either regime, as will be clear, since she is not welcomed by either; in fact, she is the representation of 'failure' within either system: as usual, she is an outsider even to the most liberal of promises. It is fair to say that Easton and Hardy's revolutionary and germinal[4] text *The Ethical Slut* is on the 'side' of polyamory, in the sense that the text provides so many useful ways in which to approach an ethical polyamorous lifestyle as a woman. *The Ethical Slut* sets out many possibilities for an ethical erotic life. Such a life could look like having several concurrent or consecutive long-term relationships, monogamy that does not conform (such as being in a couple that sometimes shares their bed with a mutually desirable third party), planned nights away from monogamy, orgies or solo Slut-hood.[5] These are all equally wonderful life choices, the legitimacy of which we must fight for. They also crucially, and indeed bravely and generously, provide (I am forever grateful that these authors have opened the possibility for authors like me to write about sexual ethics for women) us with multiple arguments for how polyamory rages against the idea that having sex with other people while in a relationship is wrong. This idea, as Wednesday Martin has argued, is absolutely crucial as a foundation for any truly ethical version of sexual ethics.[6]

The authors also tell us of the tantalizing and exciting possibilities for sex that is queer, sex that is not even recognizable as sex, such as the wonderful idea of 'outercourse', which uproots the centrality of penile penetration in sex and opens the body to the inherent queerness of sexual possibility.[7] Decentralizing a particular kind of sex also has the effect of decentralizing our human vision for particular kinds of relationships and hierarchies, and subverting our desire to possess people as property in the name of sexual pleasure, which is an impressive achievement. The book also reminds us that consent (in terms of consent to sexual touch, but also in relation to disclosure) rests at the heart of this version of slutty ethics. Consent in relation to disclosure means that all parties must agree to any opening-up arrangement (in whatever form it may take) for the sex to be ethical. And here is the part where the Mistress is excluded from the vast and transformative potential of being an Ethical Slut. Since her relationships are almost always undisclosed, it is the idea that a relationship must be disclosed in order to be ethical, which means she does not fit. This is why we need an 'ethical extension', perhaps even a rethinking, to even the most sex-positive sexual ethics.

I am still other

Let's consider how, by looking at what happens when Easton and Hardy directly address the Mistress in their book. So, as a Mistress I look to *The Ethical Slut*, and think shit, there is a party who has not consented to the relationship I am part of, that is, the wife. I feel shame. I feel all the things from the prologue to the start of this book. I frantically turn the pages, and I reach the page with a section entitled 'The Outside Lover', which looks like it is for me – I'm always outside, after all. I am so happy that they have acknowledged the problem of not knowing what to call me, since, of course, they don't: the whole of society doesn't want to name me. The authors rightly (and thankfully) say that a 'nonloaded word for you does not exist'.[8] I must admit I am somewhat alarmed by the somewhat backhanded compliment that precedes this: that the Mistress is a 'potentially loving, giving individual'. If I only have the potential for this and am not actually this, then this confirms my worst suspicions about myself and what society has thus far informed me. Nonetheless I am excited at what is to come. The authors go on to write the following:

> most of your time with your lover can be spent having fun. You are not expected to support your lover, nor to give up your career to stay home with the kids. On the downside, who do you call when you need a ride to the emergency room? Who do you call when you are sad or when you need support? Do you have any rights at all to your beloved's time, or is there somebody who sees you as the competition, with whom you may never speak or negotiate? While your position conveys few responsibilities, it often also carries very few rights.[9]

And I am confused. I am confused because I see all my story disappear into 'few responsibilities'. I see the challenge I bring, my revolution, my sexual kindness, reduced to competition. What I do see, though, is the acknowledgement that I have 'few rights'. The space I am given in this regime is small, because so little is known about my story, and because a Mistress is still taboo. It is impossible, within (even a sex-positive) framework that rests on consent and disclosure for me to be entitled to any ethical benefit. This is because I am, as the authors state at the start, the outsider. Such a framework reflects Kristeva and Cixous's contention (argued in Chapters 2 and 3) that women are not entitled to ethics as we conventionally understand them, since they are not made for women, especially not *other* women. The problem is that while the authors of *The Ethical Slut* rightly rage against the idea that being the 'other' is worth 'less-than' in a relationship, it is impossible for them to incorporate the Mistress since their ethical pre-occupation remains with the polyamorous structure which rests on consent in the form of disclosure. Of course, this is a valid ethical concern, yet the issue is with whom we exclude when our sole focus is upon this as a principle of inclusion within ethical entitlement. The issue is also that by insisting on disclosure, we further marginalize. We also exclude the stories which get to the heart of why disclosure has not been possible in Mistress relationships. This will mean the continued concealment of conditions which relate both to society broadly and its preoccupation with relationship hierarchy, and which relate to the qualities of the individuals involved in those relationships – in short, *ethical concerns*. Throughout *The Ethical Slut*, we never quite reach the threshold of finding the Mistress entitled to ethical treatment. What we do find, though, is that the wife or partner ought to be grateful for the sex-positive intervention the Mistress brings when her partner reveals their cheating behaviour.[10]

The cheat

Until Wednesday Martin's *Untrue*, it felt as though it took a special kind of bad woman to be a cheater, since good women just don't, right? Women are the faithful, naturally monogamous ones and men are the naturally sexual, restless ones, who just can't help it. A man who does it is bad enough, but a woman! Outrageous. And the woman who is the one with whom he cheats? Well, we know what happens to her. Yet, as Martin has found, women are just as hormonally driven to want sex as men, and just as likely to seek better sex and better orgasms, and can be just as selfish. As Martin says, they are being themselves, and these are facets of women's sexuality.[11] The problem at the moment is that collectively we believe that infidelity is somehow spectacular for a woman; that she is not being what she 'should' be. And here we have the clash. Sex positivity in the manner of *The Ethical Slut* compels us to reclaim our desire (which we absolutely should) but then tells us to do so ethically in a way that for many women is out of step with their inherent sexuality, or with their position within the relationship hierarchy, as is the case with the Mistress.

'Cheating', as a word, must go. As it currently stands in monogamous cultures, to cheat means to have sex with another person other than your partner; it is to mean you are a bad person. Of course you can also cheat in polyamorous structures, where the particular rules for a particular polycule or arrangement are not respected.[12] Whereas actually, you are just being yourself. As Martin writes, the reasons women cheat (and she is focusing on women in marriages or long-term partnerships) are varied: it could be that they want better sex, want to have sex with another person, are bored, unhappy in their marriage, hold money and power that provides opportunity, they have a sexual personality, or perhaps they live in a society where monogamy is not an option, or because they simply feel like it.[13]

Disclosure

Polyamory is a form of what is often called 'ethical non-monogamy' which obviously causes us the issue that any form of non-monogamy not falling within a particular ethical code is going to be unethical, and situate those within those relationships as unethical, and, at the very least, exposed to scrutiny. Perhaps this would be 'good' scrutiny if it were aimed at those who have Mistresses, who perhaps might need to work on their sexual kindness reciprocation, but, of course, it is not: the scrutiny is again directed at the Mistress, while all the while not including her within our ethical frameworks. We are faced with a perpetual cycle of exclusion and at the centre of this is the idea of 'disclosure.'

I have cheated many times. For me, cheating has been a survival strategy. Now, I am not saying that it is a strategy that has not hurt me, or others. For 20 years I was in and out of abusive relationships, and as a result of the most coercive and emotionally, psychologically, sexually, spiritually and physically violent of them, I now live with anxiety and complex PTSD. I am grateful now to be healing and to be surrounded by love, but for a long time I was in survival mode. I needed to be out. I needed to find home, and every time I thought I had, it was unsafe. During this time, I thought I was with perfectly normal, even desirable, men, and as we know from the landmark works of authors such as Judith Herman, this is indeed how they seem, and how science believes these men to be.[14] Throughout these relationships I tried to run from them by sleeping with other partners, or at least wanting to. I was trying to survive, but I was also being a cheat, and, as it happens, a Mistress, on many occasions. I could not disclose my relationships to my long-term partners, because it may have literally put my life at risk; or rather, my traumatized brain and body were doing what they needed to do to keep me alive and get me out of those situations.[15] This may have not been the healthiest strategy, but it was the only power I believed I had, and my only agency at that time. Not all Mistresses are traumatized, but I was and there will be many who are, just as there are many people living with trauma who hold different roles and identities within society. The point I am moving towards is that being asked to disclose is not always realistic. It might well be preferable, or it might be safer than it appears to be a Mistress, but against the background we have considered together over the previous chapters, it is at least understandable that a Mistress might not be able to. Yet, sex-positive sexual ethics as they are would find her unethical in the moment when she most needs sexual kindness – the moment where she is required to disclose, or the moment she is revealed. She is given no ethical support in the course of her survival, but rather shamed. Such mandatory disclosure that tends to be required of the Mistress in order that she may be entitled to ethical treatment, can as Martin writes, seem 'ethical and principled', yet remain a form of puritanical social control that forces you to confess in order to repent for your sins, while you are sinning.[16] As such, sex-positive ethical standards can be deeply unethical. Sometimes, disclosure is just not safe and being able to disclose, feeling safe enough to be able to, is a privilege that most Mistresses simply do not have, for as we have seen, our society does not form a safe and ethical space with which to receive this disclosure.

Structural double-outsider

The romance of the affair is irresistible. It can be irresistible to both the Mistress and her lover. The affair can be many things – it can be romance and excitement that is needed against the background of an old relationship, it can be the escape needed against the background of abuse, it can be the fortification of an existing relationship in a looser monogamous or non-monogamous relationship structure or it could just be because of straight up unrelenting desire that requires satisfying. The affair could be yet another turbulent swirl of the 'whirlpool'. Whatever it is, the affair, and the Mistress, will be met with the fear and suspicion which we are accustomed to by now. It is also true that we can read as many books on polyamory as we can make time for, but we will not find an ethical framework that fits the Mistress, because she is simply not who these frameworks are meant for.

We already know that the Mistress needs sexual kindness. But what I seek to add here is yet another dimension. Sexual kindness must understand that polyamory and disclosure are not necessarily, and not yet, the answer. Sexual kindness must therefore be conscious of this yet further 'othering' – the Mistress is the 'other woman,' even to sex-positivity. What the Mistress needs is kindness not a lesson on non-monogamy and how to be an ethical slut. We must remember too, that it might be that she is perfectly happy being a Mistress, and actually, she might see herself as monogamous, or what I call a 'faithful Mistress.' There is no doubt in reading Nin's *Henry and June* that Miller and Nin the Mistress extraordinaire have forged their own version of monogamy between them. Their sexual fidelity does not necessarily remain intact, but the solidity, depth and fortitude of their connection is without doubt. It reads almost as transcendental, like the petty bothers of relationship structures are an inconvenient concern to their all-consuming, everlasting love. It is a transcendental romance that reveals its contours only through Nin's writing. It is that rare thing, which perhaps De

Beauvoir and Sartre also experienced – this soul-twisting everlasting breathlessness. One gets the sense, from reading Nin's writings, that these kinds of relationships are at once wonderful and terrible; continually hovering between something joyful and something destructive. These Mistress relationships are dodgy places, they have no rules. They sit outside of polyamory, ethical non-monogamy, and of course, monogamy. As such, they have no ethical code and tend to become a mixture of both, with the Mistress left to navigate them/it herself. Excluded by the ethical formulations of both polyamory and monogamy, there needs to be something practical for her, too.

Queer and kinky keeps the faith

This particular dimension of sexual kindness, the one that addresses the fact that she is structurally outside, needs the most careful formulation, which also holds space for growth and understanding as we hear more from Mistresses of all kinds. We know that monogamous relationships have underpinned ethical codes that hinge on notions of what is objectively 'right' and 'wrong;' and it is clear from what we have seen that these are not only insufficient, but harmful for being designed not to protect the Mistress, but the power that has kept Mistresses. Legal tests such as doing what is in someone's 'best interests' also do not fit, since we have seen that we have proved ourselves time and time again insufficient judges of what these are. The Mistress does not need people to speak for her, yet again. We have also seen that polyamorous ethical codes do not fit the mistress. She needs her own. We have seen that understanding her inherent queerness, and undoing our homophobia, transphobia and biphobia is an important start to building a foundation of kindness towards the Mistress. We have also seen that understanding the centrality of white supremacy and colonial underpinning of monogamous structures is crucial to knowing what is at the heart of our mistreatment of Mistresses. We have also seen that models of consent in kink can show us a way forward to open communication around sex (providing that the Mistress is sufficiently empowered to know her needs and to voice them). Sexual kindness needs all of these things. Sexual kindness to the Mistress simultaneously understands the importance of all these aspects, but is ready to let them go the moment she speaks.

Confused? Perhaps. I don't blame you – me too. The problem is Herethical in nature, and as we know from Herethics, they do not exist.[17] And as we know from Cixous and Chapter 3, when it comes to the 'other woman', we are even more stuck. We are doing something monumental together there: we are building an entire ethical code from scratch, for someone who has never had one by virtue of being outside of every single one since the beginning of ethical codes. In the following and final chapter, I build a tentative beginning to this code. I want you to see it as unfixed and ethereal, prone to and happy to collapse as soon as a Mistress desires it. It is an orgasmic code, and can happen wherever it is needed, even when the Mistress comes on the bus, as she rubs her thighs together thinking of her married lover (and/or their wife). To help us focus, in the final set of bullet points below, I set out some of the big questions that haunt our relationship with the Mistress. They are not exhaustive by any means but intended as a set of questions and/or assumptions (some of which I have encountered, or have been encountered by the Mistresses we have met during this book) to which we can apply the Mistress Manifesto that comes in the final chapter.

- Is the Mistress required to be faithful to her married/ partnered lover?

- He's cheating on his wife in order to be with her, so should we worry about her feelings/safety at all? Surely it's the wife's feelings/safety that should take priority.

- Shouldn't the aim of relationship structures and their associated ethics be to eradicate Mistresses and extra-marital relationships, rather than to support and protect them and those that are in them?

- All Mistresses are damaged. The Mistress needs help not advice about how to navigate the poorly judged relationships that she is in. If she's a Mistress, her sex drive is too developed. She's a slut and this is bad. She can never be trusted. She's a 'mate-stealer' and needs to hurt others in order to feel good. She's a dangerous woman with 'daddy issues'.

- Misogyny, racism, homophobia/biphobia/transphobia, classism and ableism are not relevant here. What is relevant is that the Mistress is hurting other people, and if she is hurt, it's her own fault. She's just a bad person and the way society is structured has nothing to do with it.

- The Mistress deserves every punishment that she gets since she's always the guilty party. She has a choice about what she does and she made a bad choice.

- You are a Mistress, and you must find a way out of this relationship as soon as possible.

- Someone you know, perhaps a friend, is a Mistress. What should you advise her? Should you advise her to stop it?

- You find out that the lover of your friend who is a Mistress is abusive.

- The Mistress you know seems to have a huge sex drive. You also suspect that she's bisexual. Due to your own biphobia, you assume that she can never be in a loving and faithful relationship with one person, since there's more than one gender.

- If only they were both open about the relationship. Should I just keep advising her to disclose the relationship to his wife? Should he not just get it all out in the open? If he doesn't, she should just tell his wife herself, or just leave. How can she treat people like this?

- A Mistress becomes pregnant. You assume she'll get an abortion, since she cannot possibly be mother material, since she's clearly not wife material.

- Should he stay or go? Should she stay or go? Whatever they decide will tell us what kind of people they are. We'll be proven right about the way in which the world is divided.

Story Part VI: The untold story

There's no story here, yet. We need to create a new one. I'm tired of all this judgement, aren't you? It's as old as time, yet I think we can do better, kinder. This is the perfect opportunity to do so, since we've seen that he did not leave her. The call never came, and she sits alone, frozen in time. Her hand rests upon her dark and silent phone. She stares at it numbly. She doesn't yet cry, because she hasn't yet remembered all the waiting judges who want to tell her, 'I told you so' and that it's now time to move on and do better, be better. They will want to tell her that he must be with his wife now, and really this is for the best, or worse, that it's justice. She thinks of him at home. She wonders if it's a warzone, full of rows, or if it's a place of calm. Perhaps it's a destroyed nest waiting to repair, in the wake of his promise that it's over with her, and that he'll try again to be a better husband. The latter is too painful for her just now.

She awakens her phone, checks it again, still nothing. She inhales an expansive breath, a restorative one. She's survived, again. She can sense the familiarity of yet another rebirth on the horizon. She, again, in her hopeless humanity, hopes for better – this time, let's give it to her.

6

The Mistress Manifesto

The virtues of sexual kindness

Preamble: Mistress Ethics can be benevolent, kind, aroused, against ownership, possession and control, and in tune with the sexuality, diversity, but also able to understand the ethical needs of women's bodies, and the ways in which relationships under patriarchy can harm women. The Mistress is all too aware of the oppression, violence and sexual denial which have also been part of Mistress's (and other women's) lives. It turns out that the body of the Mistress and her extra-marital sex are fertile ground for generating ethics of sexuality for the future. Let's try and write them. I'll begin with seven key foundations; the Mistress, with your help and sexual kindness, must do the rest.

1. Give her a room of her own. At the core of this book is the message that we need to be brave enough to listen to the Mistress. Seek her out so that you can hear her story. Be curious. Listen like your life depends on it. Give her space to talk, a space to give and receive. Let her talk. Give her what she has never had – a room of her own. I have gestured throughout this book to Woolf's essay which is based on two lectures she gave in the late 1920s, *A Room of One's Own*, which lays the foundation of the need for women to have a space to tell their stories.[1] This space Woolf argues for is literal, but also literary in that it requires the reattribution of power to women to narrate their own stories. The queerness of Woolf's text is also of particular importance, since it has been claimed (by Jane Marcus) that Woolf was seeking – driven by her affair with her own Mistress, Vita Sackville-West – to advise her audience how to conceal references to lesbian sex without potentially appearing in an obscenity trial, as was Oscar Wilde's fate.[2] For the Mistress, claiming space in the world and on the page is hard and it can be dangerous. It is particularly hard for Black Mistresses, Mistresses of colour, trans Mistresses, working-class Mistresses and disabled Mistresses, and indeed Mistresses that embody any and all of these axes of oppression. The otherness of the Mistress can be more than double, and this directly translates into the difficulty she will experience in accessing a space to write, whether physical and/or narrative. This step is at the head of the Mistress Manifesto, since it is at the heart of how to arrive at the answers to the questions above, and how we begin to build the Mistress's wild, strengthening and radical sexual Herethics. This step tells us that we must listen before we create. This is a radical listening, though, that listens to the stories of harm that might be difficult to hear, and that might implicate us. It will be hard to hear that we have caused the Mistress harm, but deeply listening; to her voice, her body and her story is the most crucial step. To do this, we need to get comfortable with the Mistress having power to narrate her story, like Winterson's narrator and protagonist in *Written on the Body* – one of few novels giving voice to the Mistress's secret and silenced cry.[3] We need Mistress-literature. Some of the stories you hear might be fuck-filled juicy vignettes that cause a twitch of the cock and a hardening of the vulva, an awakening wherever we might feel desire. This is OK. Some of them might be stories of pain and abuse, and cause you to cry. The main thing is not to allow the stories to slip away, silenced and unintegrated into this new ethical formulation. We need these stories so we can share the pain of our Mistresses. As Shevek says to the waiting crowd in Ursula Le Guin's *The Dispossessed,* 'It is our suffering that brings us together... We are brothers in what we share.'[4] Only by listening can we know and begin to have these open conversations about Mistress relationships and Mistress sex – this is also how we begin to build the 'sexy safety' that caters for the particular risks to which the Mistress's 'othered' sexuality and her necessary adventures expose her.

2. *Sexual kindness is always unexpected.* Being kind to a Mistress might feel wrong to the structures within which we live. Just as being kind to a sex worker might, too. Being kind to a nurse does not. As we know from ethicists such as Lorde and hooks, Deleuze and Guattari, Kristeva and Cixous, kindness that makes the 'other' stronger is always discouraged by structures that oppress. But as the Mistress shows us, it is where kindness feels hardest to give that it must be given. It is also particularly when sex enters our ethical equations, as it does with Mistresses, as it does with sex workers, we find it much harder to be kind, make it through our own baggage and see the whole of the humanity of the person before us – their joys, their pleasures, their humour, their tears and their suffering. Even between women it can be hard to lean into that camaraderie we feel, and allow it to flood our bodies, but if we did, we would find all sorts of

treasures. Not least, we can access that extraordinary power of Lorde's erotic, and find ourselves connected to one another, so that we might rage alongside the Mistress in her revolution. Joining the revolution is sexual kindness, but also justice. Remember, her freedom is your freedom – our fates are conjoined.

3. *Do not judge, lest ye be judged.* Being a Mistress can be extraordinary, as much as it can be horrific. We only need to hear the stories (see Step 1 above). The stories we have heard, and in this I include my own, attest to the need for the kindness to be as orgasmic as the sex can (sometimes) be. In fact, more so. Looking back at Chapter 4, we know that often placing the need for nourishment at the centre of sex can place us in a better place to judge whether it is good or bad for us. This sex might still be filthy, perhaps weird and kinky as hell, or it might be vanilla and cosy. For the Mistress, we often assume she is having amazing sex, or that sex is at the forefront of her agenda, as opposed the nourishment of her body. Assuming that, in fact, it is nourishment that we seek when we fuck can lead us to be kinder and to have sex that is more pleasurable. This is radical stuff when we think about having a conversation of this tenor with the Mistress, since it is a conversation about *her needs* – and this is just not what happens given that her needs are not considered important due to how far she is away from 'legitimate' concern.

We know from Nin's letters and accounts, particularly in *Henry and June*, that being a Mistress can be at once intense and illuminating, powerful and debilitating. The strengths of these peaks and troughs can only be rivalled by the relationships themselves. Yet there is something to capture here and take forward. Simply put, it is an ability to be ultra-present. bell hooks tells us that a bond stronger

than death comes from recognizing what love is calling us to do –
not to fall in love but to look inward, towards ourselves.[5] This is an
especially powerful call when it comes to Mistress relationships,
being Herethical and making the body of the Mistress stronger,
instead of weaker. By approaching relationships as something to be
celebrated, by virtue of the call to enter into deeper relationships
with ourselves, we celebrate the opportunity to be kinder. This takes
us away from notions of ownership, individualism and 'good and
bad' that pervade our ethical conundrums, instead focusing us on
the question of what – as a Mistress, or someone who is thinking
of counselling or judging a Mistress – judgements do I bring to the
question of this relationship? Here we find the demand to commit
to love itself as transformative, and the possibility of being made
bold and courageous.[6] We are thus empowered by the existence of
connection itself, to love harder. For sexual kindness as something
unique to the Mistress, a crucial part of using it to develop an ethical
framework for her, it is crucial we turn inward to ourselves in the
course of understanding her. Because there is nothing else that she
ought (justly) to be judged against, all you have is her and you. Begin
with love, and you will find sexual kindness. You must overreach
in your kindness, because you must reach past all of the things that
find her doubly other, and find her, in you: your Herethical Mommy
(and/or Daddy).

   4. *Let her queer you.* Being a Mistress is queer. It is queer because
it throws straightness, and all its structures into confusion, but it
is also often queer because of the sexual closeness of all the bodies
involved in the relationship, even if this is simply a question of
proximity and accidentally shared fluids. Sometimes it might be

because the relationship is some kind of triad, like June, Henry and Anaïs, or it might otherwise be through a spectrum of erotic draw between Mistress and wife. At the core of what the Mistress does is the Herethical, in that what she does is intimately connected to others of all genders and sexualities – she is queer, and she is uniquely ethically generative. She is extraordinary in all ways, but particularly so in what she produces in terms of opportunities to be sexually kinder. If Herethics are what we place at the centre of what is good, then she is the most virtuous. As we see in Nin's writing, and the writing of many Mistresses, with this (often painful) position comes a unique opportunity to be a Spy in the House of Love,[7] and report what is known, rather than what is understood. As the gender-queering pharmaco-fucking pioneer Paul Preciado told us, we must create a 'headless philosophy' – one that values the body's experience over what the head analyses to be true. This must be a new morality, no longer based on the proclamations of the philosophical cis-heteropatriarchy.[8] The Mistress's queer Herethical body is where we must begin the philosophy that underpins her ethics. In doing so, we will answer questions differently by focusing on her as a pioneer as opposed to a threat, and someone from whom we can learn, rather than someone to whom we apply the philosophy of men, many of whom have kept (as opposed to held) Mistresses. She is a philosophy-maker and canon-fucker.

5. *Think big and reach for the future, but remember the cruelty of her history.* Reading this book will have shown you a different side of her life. It is a view from the inside, and from many different angles. You will also have seen the multiple historical (and contemporary) ways in which her story has been distorted and untold, as well as

occasionally told. Love a Mistress, fuck a Mistress, nourish her and *hold her*. In holding her, remember to understand and respect her past. Move with it as if you are trying to heal it. Understand your part in it. This is sexual kindness. Perhaps, like me, she is a serial Mistress – Mistress through and through, with many rebirths, like Mukherjee's heroine, Jasmine. Knowing that you know that will make her feel as though this is not yet another thing for her to survive. This is revolutionary love that it is fitting for someone revolutionary. This follows Lorde's demand to connect with the power of the erotic as something that can bring about change, and unlike those in power, be unafraid of it. Such a sexual kindness remembers oppression and power, though, and remembers that the Mistress does not enter the relationship holding it. Remember that you are operating in an unknown, unchartered space that is outside the law, outside what we know, outside of monogamy, non-monogamy and even relationship anarchy. Treat this as a journey into the vacuum that is outer-space. Give the power back to her, or try. Talk about it. Let her talk about it. Hold space for this conversation and love the opportunity it gives you to nourish her. Love how incredible this makes the next fuck you and she share.

6. *Don't be logical.* Let's be clear – binaries regarding gender and proscriptions as to who we can and cannot fuck are resolutely based on white supremacy and colonialism. It is also the case that it will be Black Mistresses, particularly Black trans Mistresses who will be most at risk from the danger that these colonial legacies cause. It is a matter of life and death for some Mistresses, and we must understand this in order to make the world safer. We need to listen to authors such as Mikki Kendall and Ome'seke Tinsley,[9] and songs such as WAP,[10]

to understand the voices we are missing from our philosophies of sexuality; listen and make them our canon. We need to listen to Octavia Butler when she tells us to always foreground humanity. When we read works such as these, we understand that the will to possess the Mistress, as much as the will to take a wife, is rooted in colonialism. When we understand this, we understand something different and unified about the roles of Mistress and wife: both are effective means for power to control, and to abuse, women. That is not to say that all Mistresses, nor all wives, are abused – simply that the roles themselves are effective tools should power be so minded. The wife, at least, has some security in most cases afforded by law and rules of property, family and inheritance law; the Mistress does not. Here we begin to see the injustice and futility of comparing the plight of the Mistress and wife, as well as the unfairness of our persistent assertion that it is the wife who has been done the most wrong. Of course she has been done wrong, but as the old adage has it, two wrongs do not make a right. Being sexually kind to the Mistress does not mean we must be unkind to the wife. It is possible to do both, but we must bear in mind that we are somewhat behind, centuries behind, in the debt we owe the Mistress in this respect. The idea that concerns must compete, or that there is a logical way through the problem which holds the most entitled one as the winner, or that there should be a winner at all, stems from colonialism's need to conquer. Let us not be racist; let us not be logical; let us be kind. If in doubt, return to Step 1 above.

7. *Be daring, keep her safe.* As we know from Chapter 4, sexy safety is an important part of sexual kindness. Even in the kinkiest forms of sex, there tends to be, or should be, a negotiated safety. Given the

forms of risk apparent such as emotional risk, as well as physical and sexual, and I would add structural, there is a great need for a conversation around safety and sex. That does not mean 'safe sex' in the conventional sense, although, of course, this will be part of it, but safety that is arousing. The tendency is to expect that the Mistress is strong enough, knows what she is getting into, with such a high sex drive, that these conversations are not necessary. These things might all be true of your Mistress, but they may not; and why not be daring, and ask anyway? It is the minimum a Mistress should be able to expect. Keep her safe, but also keep her well, and give her what she wants. She is precious. We know that sexual kindness is revolutionary, and to give her sexual kindness is just that; but she has been giving sexual kindness for as long as there have been Mistresses, and for as long as there has been literature. She is the revolutionary. bell hooks tells us that to embrace a 'love ethic', and all that it can do for us, we have to be courageous: 'our fear may not go away, but it will not stand in the way'.[11] Loving a revolutionary like the Mistress, especially within these times when we still fear her, will always bring about fear and prejudices inside us. I still hear those whispers rising from within myself. But these whispers need not scare us; rather, they can push us towards love – of her, of ourselves. The Mistress often lives a 'daring' sexual life, and is viewed always through her sexuality. Sexual kindness as an ethical foundation reminds us to bring kindness to the questions that involve sexuality. Sexual kindness reminds us that rather than allowing sexuality to frighten us into the judgement to which we are prone to retreat, feeding the ideas that keep her down and make her weaker; we must dare to make her stronger, to love her *more*.

Mistress Ethics

It is my hope that in reading the beginnings of this Mistress Manifesto, it could cause your answers to the questions at the end of Chapter 5 to change. Even if they might not change (perhaps they did not need to), there might at least be the generation of a new and kind romance with your Mistress. When I say, 'your Mistress', I mean the one in your heart, or of course, the one you know, or the one you have. My hope is that a little more sexual kindness seeps into the judgements we make, and then it will be spread. Sexual kindness is highly infectious, and once you give it, you will often receive – as with the hottest of fucks, there is always a bit of switching around. Sexual kindness is versatile too.

There are many stories about the Mistress, but not by her. Stories by Black Mistresses, Mistresses of colour and trans Mistresses are even more hard to come by. This is because speaking is not safe, because of all that we have learnt, and more that we need to learn. In writing this book, I want to contribute to forging a space that is *just* for her and the development of *her* ethics – the ethics she has never had. This is the first step in sexual kindness. Given the courageous work done by feminists, particularly Black feminists and feminists of colour, and all the extraordinary flights taken towards a sex-positive ethics for women, the Mistress has reason to be optimistic about her future. She also has reasons to still feel unsafe, given how she continues to be excluded by the very regimes she thought might offer promise. This has been hurtful, and it has been tiring. We have learnt, however, that by drawing on the most radical thinking, we can formulate a version of sexual kindness that might not only open up a space for her stories but allow us to love her with courage. We have learnt from Chapter 1 that sexual kindness is not simply nice but revolutionary and orgasmic. Underpinned by the thinking of revolutionaries such as Audre Lorde, Gilles Deleuze and Felix Guattari, we have a concept founded in the fundamental power of the erotic (to which the Mistress is always close, or made to be close), which actively fights the (white, colonial, male) power that fears it, and which makes bodies stronger, rather than weaker. Given both of these elements, we find a concept that mirrors women's sexuality and the orgasmic vulva – the revolution sometimes happens in secret places, and it can be relentless and unexpected to those who fear it, or hope that it stays out of sight. Sexual kindness is powered by women's sexuality. The Mistress embodies it, but she does not always receive it. The task of giving it to her, though, is both crucial and hard, given what we learnt in Chapter 2. The Mistress is already the 'other woman' by virtue of being inherently an outsider. This outsider status will then 'stick' to the identities she holds, whether it is her race, gender, sexuality, class and/ or disability. She can often be punished by those that keep her, who are often those in power (they might be royalty, politicians, philosophers, intellectuals or perhaps they hold high office within corporations or religious institutions). Power keeps Mistresses, and by virtue of its process of 'othering' her, asks society to do the same. Her 'other womanhood' derives also from the threat she poses to constructions of motherhood. Since in our minds she is not wife material, how can she be seen as mother material? As Chapter 2 tells us, she is, in fact, the perfect mother. The Mistress is a 'Herethical Body', which on the basis of Kristeva's ethical formulation means her fate is uniquely and intimately tied to the fate of others. What happens to her has a direct impact on the relationship she is in, and what she does with her body, which, unlike in conventional monogamous relationships, has a direct intimate impact on a range of (often hidden) others. This ethical status situates sexual kindness outside of polyamorous ethics, due to the undisclosed nature of the Mistress's relationship. This intimate connection with other bodies can sometimes take the form of literal intimacy with the partner of a married lover, such as with the Mistress extraordinaire, Anaïs Nin. It can also be indirect, in the form of body fluids and smells, the actual sharing of a body. As we learn in Chapter 3, this gives an inherent queerness, sometimes bisexuality (depending on the gender identities of those involved) to a Mistress. Her queerness provides yet another dimension to sexual kindness. As we learn from Helene Cixous, and from Sara Ahmed, it is the risk that she embodies, combined with her queerness, *that makes things happen.* The Mistress is never still, and is forever pushing for something else, pushing at hierarchies and relationships, just by virtue of being. This is an extraordinary virtue. Fucking is also how she asks for change. We learn too that the Mistress is always in solidarity with sex workers,[12] since she might well be one, but also, she knows all too well that sexuality as an outsider is work. We also learn that a Mistress is kinky, whether or not she actually is. The problem is that she is not necessarily endowed with the power and negotiating possibilities around consent that can come with being part of the kink community. The Mistress takes all kinds of risks, as we learn in Chapter 4, which tend to be driven by, but not necessarily met by, sexual kindness. The risks she takes are unavoidable, but unacknowledged, due to the fear and judgement that surround her relationships, and because these relationships tend to be undisclosed. Because she is so far outside, she is deemed unworthy of ethical treatment, even by the most positive of sexuality regimes, as we see in Chapter 5. Sexual kindness must also fight things that look like, or like sex-positive ethics profess, to be, but are not necessarily, on her side. This is a tough additional demand. Sexual kindness is all about fighting what hurts the Mistress, and fighting what makes us complicit. Throughout this book, particularly through the bullet points and stories, I have offered an alternative reality, a Mistress presence which sits alongside our thinking, gently, yet full of rage, asking that we listen. Our thinking, and our sexual kindness, must meet hers, if we are to build an ethical future for our relationships, of all kinds.

Story Part VII: Silicone Mistress

Behold: the Silicone Mistress. The magic body of your future. Hear a language you've never heard, full of ancient pains and pleasures, shining sounds and words, finally allowed to breathe. She is from a land, out beyond, yet to be seen by us. She was born there, rather than trying to get there. She is unmarked and unmade. She was not formed by anyone from here. Ideas of gender do not exist in this future place, and the idea that one can ever possess another has fallen out of fashion. Connection is the highest form of relationship, and its most advanced form can only be reached with a Mistress, who is the most prized and revered of all partners. She, like all of us by this time, is a gender-fluid being, who morphs along with her partner, according to what they both need. It's a transitory relationship that one finds when they are ready. But it can also last forever.

The Silicone Mistress has permanent access to The Library of Mistresses, and within it, a room of her own. In this library are all the stories gathered from the Mistresses before her. The Library of Mistresses is huge, much larger than the Library of Wives. One of the first silicone Mistresses undertook some research and found some stories were repeated in both libraries, and some Mistresses became wives, and wives became Mistresses. Power was outlawed from keeping Mistresses, unless whoever held the power spent a year in The Library of Mistresses reading, listening and viewing stories. Right and wrong, better and worse became outdated – almost quaintly amusing concepts that fell out of use. Before having a Mistress, or in fact, any relationship at all, every person had to attend an Orgasma-School, where as well as learning the spoken and written tongue of the Mistress, they learn the art and philosophy (and it was now considered the very highest form of both) of sexual kindness and its virtues. Silicone Mistresses are the teachers and the classrooms are hotel rooms, but with not a single polyester bed runner in sight.

NOTES

Prologue

1 Here I am referring to Dossie Easton and Janet Hardy's landmark sex-positive ethical code, *The Ethical Slut* (Easton, Dossie and Janet Hardy, *The Ethical Slut* (Ten Speed Press, [1997] 2017), which is a particularly useful starting point for those contemplating or already pursuing non-monogamous relationship formations, and to which I return in Chapters 1 and 5.

Chapter 1

1 Smart, Elizabeth, *By Grand Central Station I Sat Down and Wept* (Flamingo, [1945] 1992) p96.

2 Ibid at p97.

3 See Sollée, Kristen, *Witches, Sluts, Feminist: Conjuring the Sex Positive* (Stone Bridge Press, 2017) p19, and regarding the historical foundation of society's compulsion and multiple unsuccessful attempts to control and subsequently punish sexuality, particularly women's sexuality, see Berkowitz, Eric, *Sex and Punishment: Four Thousand Years of Judging Desire* (Counterpoint, 2012). See also how the 'wildness' within women has been persistently suppressed, meaning so too has women's inherent creativity and the life-giving messages of their souls – particularly when we consider the multiple ways in which the Mistress is an outsider, in the classic Estes, Pinkola, Clarissa, *Women Who Run with the Wolves: Myths and Stories of the Wild Woman Archetype* (Ballantine Books, 1989).

4 Butler, Octavia, *The Parable of the Sower* (Headline Publishing, [1993] 2019).

5 Smart, *By Grand Central Station I Sat Down and Wept,* p103 (emphasis in the original).

6 Ibid at p112.

7 Moss, Elizabeth, *Signs for Lost Children* (Granta Kindle Edition, 2015). location 4369.

8   Manne, Kate, *Down Girl: The Logic of Misogyny* (Penguin, 2019) p119.

9   Story, Joseph as cited in Angert, Eugene, 'The Law Is Not a Jealous Mistress', *The Virginia Law Register, The Virginia Law Review*, 12:10 (1927) pp577–93, p578.

10   Adultery is a ground for divorce in many jurisdictions, including the UK and US, and refers to penis in vagina sex with a person on the 'opposite' sex. If the extra-marital sex is not penis in vagina, it cannot be adultery (though it could be unreasonable behaviour).

11   See Gutting, Gary, *Foucault: A Very Short Introduction* (Oxford University Press, 2019) and/or Foucault, Michel, *History of Sexuality I: The Will to Knowledge* (Penguin, 2019).

12   See Valenti, Jessica, *The Purity Myth: How America's Obsession with Virginity Is Hurting Young Women* (Seal Press, 2010).

13   Atwood, Margaret, *The Handmaid's Tale* (Vintage, 1996).

14   See the disturbingly recent UK (English) case of *R v R* [1991] UKHL 12.

15   Davis, Angela Y., *Women, culture and politics* (Vintage Books, 1984) p127.

16   The family no longer denies the relationship. See Farah Stockman's article in the *New York Times* (2018): 'Monticello Is Done Avoiding Jefferson's Relationship with Sally Hemmings' retrieved from https://www.nytimes.com/2018/06/16/us/sally-hemings-exhibit-monticello.html

17   Tinsley, Omise'eke, *Beyoncé in Formation: Remixing Black Feminism* (University of Texas Press, 2018).

18   See Ibid. and a Bhandar, Brenna and Rafeef Ziadah (eds) *Revolutionary Feminisms* (Verso, 2020).

19   See Iantaffi, Alex, *Gender Trauma: Healing Cultural, Social and Historical Trauma* (Jessica Kingsley Publishers, 2020) for extensive and trauma informed analysis on this point.

20   See Benard, Akeia, 'Colonizing Black Female Bodies Within Patriarchal Capitalism: Feminist and Human Rights Perspectives', *Sexualization, Media and Society* (2019). Online First, https://journals.sagepub.com/doi/full/10.1177/2374623816680622

21   Ibid.

22   See the landmark legal feminist text Hunter, Rosemary et al (eds) *Feminist Judgments: From Theory to Practice* (Bloomsbury Professional, 2010) for various ways in which actual judgements in UK legal cases in the field of

family and criminal law (fields in which legal personhood is persistently denied to women) could be re-written from a feminist perspective in order to both criticize the way the law does not listen to women or tends to hold to stereotypes, and to think through ways of treating women as full persons before the law.

23 Richardson, Samuel, *Pamela: On Virtue Rewarded* (Oxford World Classics, [1741] 2001).

24 Bancroft, Lundy, *Why Does He Do That? Inside the Minds of Angry and Controlling Men* (Berkley, 2003).

25 Davis, *Women, culture and politics*, p14.

26 Benioff, David, Weiss, D, Strauss, Carolyn, Doelger, Frank, Caulfield, Bernadette, Cogman, Bryan, Sapochnik, Miguel and Nutter, David (Executive Producers) (2011–2019) *Game of Thrones* [TV Series] (Season 4 episode 10) HBO Entertainment, HBO.

27 Easton, Dossie and Janet Hardy, *The Ethical Slut* (Ten Speed Press, [1997] 2017).

28 Ibid at p1.

29 Sollée, *Witches, Sluts, Feminist*, p81.

30 Martin, Wednesday, *Untrue* (Scribe Publications, 2018) p19.

31 Ibid.

32 Ibid at p4.

33 I found that great explainer/texts to accompany initial forays into Deleuze and Guattari's often bewildering (yet, I maintain, magical) work are Colebrook, Claire, *Deleuze: A Guide for the Perplexed* (Continuum, 2006) and/or Colebrook, Claire, *Understanding Deleuze* (Routledge, 2002). If you prefer to jump straight into the Body without Organs, then the place to go is Deleuze, Gilles and Felix Guattari, *A Thousand Plateaus*, trans. B. Massumi (Continuum, 2004).

34 See Deleuze and Guattari, *A Thousand Plateaus* and see also the excellent Introduction (and chapters) in Beckman, Frida (ed), *Deleuze and Sex* (Edinburgh University Press, 2011) for a way of thinking through the possibilities of the Body without Organs for ways of re-imagining human sexuality.

35 See Brooks, Victoria, 'Deleuze and Guattari Got the Female Orgasm Wrong', *Institute of Arts and Ideas* (2020). Retrieved from https://iai.tv/articles/deleuze-and-guattari-got-the-female-orgasm-wrong-auid-1311

36 Jagose, Annamarie, *Orgasmology* (Duke University Press, 2012).

37 See Deleuze, G, *Spinoza: Practical Philosophy*, trans. R. Hurley (City Lights Publishers, 2001).

38 Kristeva, Julia, trans. Goldhammer, Arthur, 'Stabat Mater', *Poetics Today*, 6:1/2 (1985) pp133–52, p151.

39 Nin, Anaïs, *A Spy in the House of Love* (Penguin Classics, [1954] 2001) p24.

40 Baker, Nicholson, *Vox* (Granta, 1992).

41 See Brooks, Victoria, *Fucking Law: The Search for Her Sexual Ethics* (Zero Books, 2019).

42 Phipps, Alison, *Me Too, Not You* (Manchester University Press, 2020) p82.

43 See Ibid. and see Bhandar and Ziadah (eds) *Revolutionary Feminisms* for a variety of abolitionist texts, and Vitale, Alex, *The End of Policing* (Verso, 2017).

44 See Sollée, *Witches, Sluts, Feminist: Conjuring the Sex Positive*.

45 Lorde, Audre, 'Uses of the Erotic', in Audre Lorde (ed), *Sister Outsider* (Ten Speed Press, [1984] 2016).

46 Ibid at p90.

47 Ibid at p89, emphasis in the original.

48 hooks, bell, *all about love* (HarperCollins, 2001) pp85–103.

49 Lorde, 'Uses of the Erotic', p90.

50 Cave, Nick and the Bad Seeds (1986) Stranger than Kindness [Song] on *Your Funeral... My Trial*, Mute.

51 See The Mirror's report, Kindon, Frances (July 2020) 'Inside Johnny Depp and Vanessa Paradis' Tragic Split before Amber Heard "seduced" Him' retrieved from https://www.mirror.co.uk/3am/celebrity-news/inside-johnny-depp-vanessa-paradis-22322199

52 See The Law Society Gazette's report of the case of Depp's case against News Group Newspapers which concerned the term 'wife beater' used by the paper in relation to Depp's wife and former Mistress, Amber Heard: The Law Society Gazette (November 2020) 'Libel and Slander: Defamatory Words' retrieved from https://www.lawgazette.co.uk/law-reports/libel-and-slander-defamatory-words/5106612.article

53 Abbott, E, *Mistresses: A History of the Other Woman* (Duckworth Overlook) p327.

Chapter 2

1   See the preface and chapters one and two of Taddeo, Lisa, *Three Women* (Bloomsbury, 2019).

2   Mundell, Claire, Elizabeth Kilgarriff and Gaynor Holmes (executive producers) (2018) *The Cry* [TV Series] Episode 2, Synchronicity Films, ABC, BBC One.

3   Griffin, Victoria, *The Mistress: Histories, Myths and Interpretations of the 'other woman'* (Bloomsbury, 1999) and see the review by Weaver, Courtney, 'My Darling Concubine' Books, *The New York Times* (1999). Retrieved from https://archive.nytimes.com/www.nytimes.com/books/99/12/05/reviews/991205.05weavert.html.

4   Coel, Michaela, Phil Clarke, Roberto Troni, Sam Miller and Jo McLellan (executive producers) (2020) *I May Destroy You* [TV Series] Episode 8, Various Artists Limited and FALKNA Productions, BBC One, HBO.

5   Satrapi, Marjane (Director) *Radioactive* [Film] Working Title Films and Shoebox Films.

6   Sollée, *Witches, Sluts, Feminist: Conjuring the Sex Positive*, p45–56.

7   Woolf, Virginia, *A Room of One's Own* (Stronck Press, 2013) p61.

8   Supra, n59.

9   Ibid at p23.

10 Origin Pictures and Cité-Amérique (2011) *The Crimson Petal and the White* [TV Series] BBC Two.

11 Smart, *By Grand Central Station I Sat Down and Wept*.

12 Supra, n50.

13 Kendall, Mikki, *Hood Feminism: Notes from the Women White Feminists Forgot* (Bloomsbury, 2020).

14 See Mac, Juno and Molly Smith, *Revolting Prostitutes: The Fight for Sex Worker's Rights* (Verso, 2020).

15 Watson, Christie, *The Language of Kindness: A Nurse's Story* (Vintage, 2019).

16 Ibid at p12.

17 Kristeva, Julia trans. Goldhammer, Arthur (1985) Stabat Mater, *Poetics Today*, 6:1/2, pp133–52.

18 Ibid.

19 Winterson, Jeanette, *Written on the Body* (Vintage, [1992] 2001) p74.

20 Allen, Woody (Director) (2005) *Match Point* [Film] BBC Films.

21 Nakao, Annie (2004) 'Her tale was brutal, sexual. No one believed a slave woman could be so literate. But now Harriet Jacobs her reclaimed her name' *SF Gate*, retrieved from https://www.sfgate.com/entertainment/article/Her-tale-was-brutal-sexual-No-one-believed-a-2747114.php. See also Jacobs' diaries at Jacobs, Harriet, *Incidents in the Life of a Slave Girl* (Digireads, [1861] 2016).

22 Manne, Kate, *Down Girl: The Logic of Misogyny* (Penguin, 2019) p98.

23 Supra, n66.

24 See Snorton Riley, C. *Black on Both Sides: A Racial History of Trans Identity* (University of Minnesota Press, 2017) and Iantaffi, Alex, *Gender Trauma: Healing Cultural, Social and Historical Trauma* (Jessica Kingsley Publishers, 2020).

25 Ibid.

26 Hollibaugh, Amber, *My Dangerous Desires: A Queer Girl Dreaming Her Way Home* (Duke University Press, 2000) p16.

27 Ibid at p12.

28 Ibid at p17.

29 Parton, Dolly (1973) Jolene [Song] *Jolene*, RCA Victor.

30 Walker, Alice, *The Color Purple* (Phoenix, [1982] 2017).

31 Ibid at p81.

32 Ibid at p78.

33 See Valenti, Jessica, *The Purity Myth: How America's Obsession with Virginity Is Hurting Young Women* (Seal Press, 2010).

34 Walker, *The Color Purple*, p79.

35 American Library Association, '100 Most Frequently Challenged Books by Decade'. Retrieved from http://www.ala.org/advocacy/bbooks/frequentlychallengedbooks/top100

36 Wilson, Ruth, Ruth Kenley-Letts, Neil Blair, Lucy Richer, Rebecca Eaton (executive producers) (2018) *Mrs Wilson* [TV Series] Snowed-In Productions, BBC One.

37 Martin, *Untrue*, p238.

38 Ibid at p237.

39 Ibid at p245.

40 Ibid at p255.

41 Ibid at p233.

42 Walters, Joanna, 'Stormy Daniels Talks About Trump and the Worst 90 Seconds of My Life on Standup Tour', *The Guardian* (2019) https://www. theguardian.com/us-news/2019/may/08/stormy-daniels-talks-about-trump-and-the-worst-90-seconds-of-my-life-on-stand-up-tour

43 *Clinton v. Jones* 520 US 681 (1997).

44 Bill Clinton – 'I Did Not Have Sexual Relations with That Woman', footage retrieved from https://www.youtube.com/watch?v=VBe_guezGGc

45 For an overview/timeline of Boris Johnson's affairs, see Sullivan, Rebecca (2020) 'The entire timeline of Boris Johnson's very, er, busy romantic history' *Now to Love* retrieved from https://www.nowtolove.com.au/news/international-news/boris-johnson-wife-girlfriend-57264

46 Manne, *Down Girl,* p111.

47 Ibid at p112.

48 Ibid at p113.

49 Supra, n25.

50 For an extensive commentary of numerous examples, see Abbott, Elizabeth, *Mistresses: The History of the Other Woman* (Clearway Logistics, 2011).

51 Derrida, On the Private Lives of Philosophers, footage retrieved from https://www.youtube.com/watch?v=bay7Wh8D-HM

52 See here for a book of letters between Heidegger and Arendt: Ludz, Ursula and Andrew Shields (eds) *Letters, 1925–1975* (Houghton Mifflin Harcourt, 2004).

53 See Van Norden, Bryan, 'Western Philosophy Is Racist', *Aeon* (2017), https://aeon.co/essays/why-the-western-philosophical-canon-is-xenophobic-and-racist See also Brooks, Victoria, 'Why We Need a New Philosophy of Sex', *The Conversation* (2019). Retrieved from https://theconversation.com/why-we-need-a-new-philosophy-of-sex-112045

54 See Varden, Helga, *Kant and Sexuality* (Palgrave Macmillan, 2017) for an excellent overview of Kant and his readings of sexuality. See also the *Stanford Encyclopaedia of Philosophy* for the philosophical 'canon's' take on sexuality, 'Sex and Sexuality' retrieved from https://plato.stanford.edu/entries/sex-sexuality/

55 For a fascinating take, see Boulé, Jean-Pierre, 'Sex with Sartre', *Institute of Arts and Ideas* (2018). Retrieved from https://iai.tv/articles/sex-with-sartre-auid-1034

56 Dryden, Jane, 'Hegel, Feminist Philosophy and Disability: Re-reading our History', *Disability Studies Quarterly*, 33:4 (2013).

57 Preciado, Paul B. *Testojunkie: Sex, Drugs and Biopolitics in the Pharmacopornographic Era* (The Feminist Press, 2013) p249.

58 See Reader, Keith, *Intellectuals and the Left in France since 1968* (Palgrave Macmillan, 1987).

59 Herman, Judith, *Trauma and Recovery: The Aftermath of Violence from Domestic Abuse to Political Terror* (Basic Books, [1992] 2015) p72–3.

60 Ibid.

61 See Brooks, Victoria, 'Why the Legal Definition of Consent Fails Victims', *The Conversation* (2019). Retrieved from https://theconversation.com/why-the-legal-definition-of-consent-fails-victims-124033

62 Supra, n112.

63 Phipps, *Me Too, Not You*.

64 Manne, *Down Girl*, p115.

65 See Bhandar and Ziadah (eds) *Revolutionary Feminisms*. In particular, see the interview with Angela Y. Davis on pp203–16 for an abolitionist approach to gender based on eradicating its colonial and racist foundations.

66 Kinouani, Guilaine, *Living While Black: The Essential Guide to Overcoming Racial Trauma* (Penguin, 2021).

67 See Tinsley, *Beyoncé in Formation*.

68 Yalom, Bianca, Julie Plovnick and Bianca Lamblin, *A Disgraceful Affair* (Northeastern University Press, 1996).

Chapter 3

1 Dibb, Saul (Director) (2008) *The Duchess* [Film] Qwerty Films and Magnolia Mae Films.

2 Ibid.

3 Nin, Anaïs, *Henry and June* (Penguin Classics, [1987] 2017) p121.

4 Ibid at p204.

5 Ibid at p213.

6 Kaufman, Philip (Director) (1990) *Henry and June* [Film] Walrus and Associates.

7 Smart, *By Grand Central Station I Sat Down and Wept*, p20.

8 Ibid.

9 Cixous, Hélène, trans. Keith Cohen and Paula Cohen, 'The Laugh of the Medusa', *Signs*, 1:4 (1976) pp875–93, p881.

10 Ibid at p893.

11 Ibid at p884.

12 Barker, Meg-John and Alex Iantaffi, *Life Isn't Binary* (Jessica Kingsley Publishers, 2019) p21.

13 Ibid at p23.

14 Ibid at p24.

15 Cixous, 'The Laugh of the Medusa', pp875–93, p893.

16 Ahmed, Sara, *Queer Phenomenology: Orientations, Objects, Others* (Duke University Press, 2006) p107.

17 Ibid.

18 Manne, *Down Girl*, p118.

19 Lorde, 'Uses of the Erotic', p88.

20 Bannerjee, Pompi, Raj Merchant and Jaya Sharma (The Kinky Collective, India), 'Kink and Feminism – Breaking the Boundaries', *Sociology and Anthropology*, 6:3 (2018) pp313–20. Retrieved from http://www.hrpub.org/download/20180228/SA4-19610736.pdf p319

21 Deleuze, Gilles and Leopold von Sacher-Masoch, *Masochism: Coldness and Cruelty in Venus in Furs*, trans. Jean McNeil (Zone Books, 1991) p16.

22 Ibid at p26.

23 Cixous, 'The Laugh of the Medusa', pp875–93, p876.

24 Winterson, Jeanette, *Written on the body* (Vintage, [1992] 2001).

25 Ibid at p120.

26 See the introduction to: Thompson, Mark et al, *Leatherfolk: Radical Sex, People, Politics and Practice* (Daedalus Publishing, 2013).

27 See The Leather Archives and Museum 'A Room of Her Own' retrieved from https://leatherarchives.org/a-room-of-her-own

28 See Court, Maddy, 'FIST is the Leatherdyke Zine You'll Want to Hold in Your Hot Little Hands' on *Into* (2018). Retrieved from https://www.intomore.com/culture/fist-is-the-leatherdyke-zine-youll-want-to-hold-in-your-hot-little-hands

29 Lane, Nicole. S., 'BDSM Subspace Explained by Someone Who Has Personally Experienced It', *Hello Flo* (2017). Retrieved from https://helloflo.com/what-is-subspace/

30 For an understanding of pleasure-centred approaches to trans sex, see Fielding, Lucie *Trans Sex: Clinical Approaches to Trans Sexualities and Erotic Embodiment* (Routledge, 2021).

31 Sollée, *Witches, Sluts, Feminist,* p98.

32 Cardi B and Megan Thee Stallion (2020) *WAP* [Song] Atlantic.

33 Brand, Russell, 'WAP with Cardi B and Megan Thee Stallion: Feminist Masterpiece or Porn?' (2020). Retrieved from https://www.youtube.com/watch?v=EdP9H60N2l8

34 See Brand, Russell, *My Booky Wook* (Hodder Paperbacks, 2008).

35 Sollée, *Witches, Sluts, Feminist.*

36 Ibid at p98.

37 Abbott, *Mistresses,* p382.

38 De Lacoste, Guillemine, 'An Intricate Relationship: Simone De Beauvoir and Bianca Lamblin,' *Simone De Beauvoir Studies*, 11:105–110 (1994) p106.

39 Ibid.

40 Ibid.

41 See for example, Maloney, Alison, 'No Woman Was Safe,' (2019). Retrieved from https://www.thesun.co.uk/tvandshowbiz/9120419/true-story-of-gentleman-jack-anne-lister/

42 See Helena, Whitbread, *The Secret Diaries of Miss Anne Lister Vol 1: Know My Own Heart*, ed Lister Anne (Virago, 2010) and Helena, Whitbread, *The*

Secret Diaries of Miss Anne Lister Vol 2: No Priest but Love, ed Lister Anne (Virago, 2020).

43 Manne, *Down Girl.*

44 Yalom, Bianca, Julie Plovnick and Bianca Lamblin, *A Disgraceful Affair* (Northeastern University Press, 1996).

45 See Brooks, 'Deleuze and Guattari got the Female Orgasm Wrong'.

46 Winterson, *Written on the body.*

47 Barker and Iantaffi, *Life isn't Binary*, p54.

48 Ibid at p59–60.

49 Ibid at p60.

50 Nelson, Maggie, *The Arganauts* (Mellville House, 2015) p16.

51 Iantaffi, Alex, *Gender Trauma: Healing Cultural, Social and Historical Trauma* (Jessica Kingsley Publishers, 2020).

Chapter 4

1 Hollibaugh, *My Dangerous Desires*, p263.

2 Baldwin, James *Munich, Winter 1973* retrieved from *The Poetry Foundation* at https://www.poetryfoundation.org/poems/88926/munich-winter-1973-for-ys

3 Lorde, Audre, *Zami: A New Spelling of My Name* (Penguin Classics, [1982] 2018) p250.

4 Butler, Octavia, *Bloodchild* (Seven Stories Press, [1995] 2005) p193.

5 See Johnston, Lynda and Robyn Longhurst, *Space Place and Sex* (Rowman and Littlefield, 2010).

6 See Horrocks, Chris and Jevtic Zoran, *Introducing Foucault: A Graphic Guide* (Icon Books, 2014) for an introduction and Taylor, Chloe, *The Routledge Guidebook to Foucault's The History of Sexuality* (Routledge, 2016).

7 hooks, *all about love*, p91 and p93.

8 Ibid at p95.

9   In terms of resources I have found helpful in combination with therapy, I would recommend Herman, *Trauma and Recovery*, Van Der Kolk, Bessel, *The Body Keeps the Score: Mind, Brain and Body in the Transformation of Trauma* (Penguin, 2015) and Levine, Peter, *In An Unspoken Voice: How the Body Releases Trauma and Restores Goodness* (Atlantic Books, 2010) for finding out about the effects of trauma.

10 hooks, *all about love*.

11 Ibid at p175.

12 Nin, Anaïs, *Eros Unbound* (Penguin, [1979] 2007).

13 Baker, Nicholson, *House of Holes* (Simon and Schuster, 2011) and Baker, Nicholson, *Vox* (Granta, 1992).

14 Roche, Charlotte, *Wetlands* (Fourth Estate, 2009).

15 Nelson, *The Arganauts*, p77.

16 Cixous, Hélène, *The Book of Promethea* (University of Nebraska Press, [1983] 1991) p152.

17 Angel, Katherine, *Daddy Issues* (Peninsula Press, 2019) p17.

18 Ibid at p27.

19 Ibid.

20 Ibid at p59.

21 Ibid at p28.

22 hooks, *all about love*, pp169–70.

23 Sollée, *Witches, Sluts, Feminist*, pp69–73.

Chapter 5

1   Lorde, Audre, 'A Litany for Survival' [1978] (1997). Retrieved from https://www.poetryfoundation.org/poems/147275/a-litany-for-survival

2   Mukherjee, Bharati, *Jasmine* (Virago, [1989] 1991) p228.

3   Winterson, Jeanette, *Written on the Body* (Vintage, [1992] 2001) p16.

4   Used to replace 'seminal' as a term masculine centred, by Angela Y. Davis in Angela, Davis Y. and Rodriguez Dylan, 'The Challenge of Prison Abolition, A Conversation', *Social Justice*, 27:3 (2000) pp212–18, p215.

5   Easton, Dossie and Hardy, Janet, *The Ethical Slut: A Guide to Infinite Sexual Possibilities* (Ten Speed Press, [1997] 2017).

6   Martin, *Untrue*.

7   Easton and Hardy, *The Ethical Slut*, p36.

8   Ibid at p187.

9   Ibid at p188.

10   Ibid at p190.

11   Martin, *Untrue*, p260.

12   Easton and Hardy, *The Ethical Slut* and also see Franklin, Veaux and Eve Rickert, *More Than Two: A Practical Guide to Ethical Polyamory* (Thorntree Press, 2014).

13   Martin, *Untrue*, p260.

14   Herman, Judith, *Trauma and Recovery: The Aftermath of Violence from Domestic Abuse to Political Terror* (Basic Books, [1992] 2015).

15   Supra, and see also van der Kolk, Bessel, *The Body Keeps the Score: Mind, Brain and Body in the Transformation of Trauma* (Penguin, 2015).

16   Martin, *Untrue*, p34.

17   See Chapter 2.

Chapter 6

1   Woolf, *A Room of One's Own*.

2   Marcus, Jane, *Virginia Woolf, Cambridge and a Room of One's Own: 'The Proper Upkeep of Names'* (Cecil Woolf Publishers, 1996) p33.

3   Winterson, *Written on the Body*.

4   Le Guin, Ursula, *The Dispossessed* (Gateway, [1974] 1999) p300.

5   hooks, *all about love*, p188.

6   Ibid at p188.

7   Nin, *Henry and June*.

8   See Preciado, Paul B., *Testojunkie: Sex, Drugs and Biopolitics in the Pharmacopornographic Era* (The Feminist Press, 2013) and see also his book outlining an extraordinary case for a planetary revolution, Preciado, Paul B., *An Apartment on Uranus*, trans. Charlotte Mandell (Fitzcarraldo Editions, 2020).

9   Supra, n16 and n66.

10 Supra, n152.

11 hooks, *all about love*, p101.

12 Mac, Juno and Smith, Molly, *Revolting Prostitutes: The Fight for Sex Worker's Rights* (Verso, 2020).

REFERENCES

Abbott, Elizabeth, *Mistresses: A History of the Other Woman* (Duckworth Overlook, 2003).

Abbott, Elizabeth, *Mistresses: The History of the Other Woman* (Clearway Logistics, 2011).

Ahmed, Sara, *Queer Phenomenology: Orientations, Objects, Others* (Duke University Press, 2006).

American Library Association, '100 Most Frequently Challenged Books by Decade', retrieved from http://www.ala.org/advocacy/bbooks/frequentlychallengedbooks/top100

Angel, Katherine, *Daddy Issues* (Peninsula Press, 2019).

Atwood, Margaret, *The Handmaid's Tale* (Vintage, 1996).

Baker, Nicholson, *House of Holes* (Simon and Schuster, 2011).

Baker, Nicholson, *Vox* (Granta, 1992).

Baldwin, James, 'Munich', *Winter* (1973), retrieved from *The Poetry Foundation* at https://www.poetryfoundation.org/poems/88926/munich-winter-1973-for-ys

Bancroft, Lundy, *Why Does He Do That? Inside the Minds of Angry and Controlling Men* (Berkley, 2003).

Bannerjee, Pompi, Merchant, Raj and Sharma, Jaya (The Kinky Collective, India), 'Kink and Feminism – Breaking the Boundaries', *Sociology and Anthropology*, 6:3 (2018), 313–20.

Barker, Meg-John and Iantaffi, Alex, *Life Isn't Binary* (Jessica Kingsley Publishers, 2019).

Benard, Akeia, 'Colonizing Black Female Bodies Within Patriarchal Capitalism: Feminist and Human Rights Perspectives', *Sexualization, Media and Society* (2019), Online First, https://journals.sagepub.com/doi/full/10.1177/2374623816680622

Beckman, Frida (ed) *Deleuze and Sex* (Edinburgh University Press, 2011).

Berkowitz, Eric, *Sex and Punishment: Four Thousand Years of Judging Desire* (Counterpoint, 2012).

Bhandar, Brenna and Ziadah, Rafeef (eds) *Revolutionary Feminisms* (Verso, 2020).

Boulé, Jean-Pierre, 'Sex with Sartre', *Institute of Arts and Ideas* (2018), retrieved from https://iai.tv/articles/sex-with-sartre-auid-1034

Brand, Russell, *My Booky Wook* (Hodder Paperbacks, 2008).

Brooks, Victoria, 'Why the Legal Definition of Consent Fails Victims', *The Conversation* (2019), retrieved from https://theconversation.com/why-the-legal-definition-of-consent-fails-victims-124033

Brooks, Victoria, 'Why We Need a New Philosophy of Sex', *The Conversation* (2019), retrieved from https://theconversation.com/why-we-need-a-new-philosophy-of-sex-112045

Brooks, Victoria, 'Deleuze and Guattari Got the Female Orgasm Wrong', *Institute of Arts and Ideas* (2020), retrieved from https://iai.tv/articles/deleuze-and-guattari-got-the-female-orgasm-wrong-auid-1311

Butler, Octavia, *Bloodchild* (Seven Stories Press, [1995] 2005).

Butler, Octavia, *The Parable of the Sower* (Headline Publishing, [1993] 2019).

Cardi B and Megan Thee Stallion (2020) *WAP* [Song] Atlantic.

Cave, Nick and the Bad Seeds (1986) Stranger than Kindness [Song] on *Your Funeral ... My Trial*, Mute.

Cixous, Hélène, trans. Cohen, Keith and Cohen, Paula, 'The Laugh of the Medusa', *Signs*, 1:4 (1976), 875–93.

Cixous, Hélène, *The Book of Promethea* (University of Nebraska Press, [1983] 1991) p152.

Colebrook, Claire, *Understanding Deleuze* (Routledge, 2002).

Colebrook, Claire, Deleuze: *A Guide for the Perplexed* (Continuum, 2006).

Court, Maddy, 'FIST Is the Leatherdyke Zine You'll Want to Hold in Your Hot Little Hands', on *Into* (2018), retrieved from https://www.intomore.com/culture/fist-is-the-leatherdyke-zine-youll-want-to-hold-in-your-hot-little-hands

Davis, Angela Y., *Women, culture and politics* (Vintage Books, 1984).

Davis, Angela Y. and Dylan, Rodriguez, 'The Challenge of Prison Abolition, A Conversation', *Social Justice*, 27:3 (2000), 212–18.

De Lacoste, Guillemine, 'An Intricate Relationship: Simone De Beauvoir and Bianca Lamblin', *Simone De Beauvoir Studies*, 11 (1994), 105–10.

Deleuze, Gilles, *Spinoza: Practical Philosophy*, trans. Hurley, R (City Lights Publishers, 2001).

Deleuze, Gilles and Guattari, Felix, *A Thousand Plateaus*, trans. Massumi, B (Continuum, 2004).

Deleuze, Gilles and Von Sacher-masoch, Leopold, *Masochism: Coldness and Cruelty in Venus in Furs*, trans. McNeil, Jean (Zone Books, 1991).

Dryden, Jane, 'Hegel, Feminist Philosophy and Disability: Re-reading Our History', *Disability Studies Quarterly*, 33:4 (2013).

Easton, Dossie and Hardy, Janet, *The Ethical Slut* (Ten Speed Press, [1997] 2017).

Fielding, Lucie, *Trans Sex: Clinical Approaches to Trans Sexualities and Erotic Embodiment* (Routledge, 2021).

Foucault, Michel, *History of Sexuality I: The Will to Knowledge* (Penguin, 2019).

Griffin, Victoria, *The Mistress: Histories, Myths and Interpretations of the 'Other Woman'* (Bloomsbury, 1999).

Gutting, Gary, *Foucault: A Very Short Introduction* (Oxford University Press, 2019).

Herman, Judith, *Trauma and Recovery: The Aftermath of Violence from Domestic Abuse to Political Terror* (Basic Books, [1992] 2015).

hooks, bell, *All About Love* (HarperCollins, 2001).

Hollibaugh, Amber, *My Dangerous Desires: A Queer Girl Dreaming Her Way Home* (Duke University Press, 2000).

Horrocks, Chris and Zoran, Jevtic, *Introducing Foucault: A Graphic Guide* (Icon Books, 2014).

Hunter, Rosemary et al (eds) *Feminist Judgments: From Theory to Practice* (Bloomsbury Professional, 2010).

Iantaffi, Alex, *Gender Trauma: Healing Cultural, Social and Historical Trauma* (Jessica Kingsley Publishers, 2020).

Jacobs, Harriet, *Incidents in the Life of a Slave Girl* (Digireads, [1861] 2016).

Jagose, Annamarie, *Orgasmology* (Duke University Press, 2012).

Johnston, Lynda and Longhurst, Robyn, *Space Place and Sex* (Rowman and Littlefield, 2010).

Kendall, Mikki, *Hood Feminism: Notes from the Women White Feminists Forgot* (Bloomsbury, 2020).

Kindon, Frances, 'Inside Johnny Depp and Vanessa Paradis' Tragic Split before Amber Heard "Seduced" Him' (July 2020), retrieved from https://www.mirror.co.uk/3am/celebrity-news/inside-johnny-depp-vanessa-paradis-22322199

Kristeva, Julia, trans. Goldhammer, Arthur, 'Stabat Mater', *Poetics Today*, 6:1/2 (1985), 133–52.

The Law Society Gazette, 'Libel and Slander: Defamatory Words' (November 2020), retrieved from https://www.lawgazette.co.uk/law-reports/libel-and-slander-defamatory-words/5106612.article

The Leather Archives and Museum 'A Room of Her Own', retrieved from https://leatherarchives.org/a-room-of-her-own

Lane, Nicole. S., 'BDSM Subspace Explained by Someone Who Has Personally Experienced It', *Hello Flo* (2017), retrieved from https://helloflo.com/what-is-subspace/

Le Guin, Ursula, *The Dispossessed* (Gateway, [1974] 1999).

Levine, Peter, *In An Unspoken Voice: How the Body Releases Trauma and Restores Goodness* (Atlantic Books, 2010).

Lorde, Audre, 'A Litany for Survival', [1978] (1997), retrieved from https://www.poetryfoundation.org/poems/147275/a-litany-for-survival

Lorde, Audre, 'Uses of the Erotic', in Lorde, Audre (ed), *Sister Outsider* (Ten Speed Press [1984] 2016).

Lorde, Audre, *Zami: A New Spelling of My Name* (Penguin Classics, [1982] 2018).

Ludz, Ursula and Shields, Andrew (eds) *Letters, 1925–1975* (Houghton Mifflin Harcourt, 2004).

Mac, Juno and Smith, Molly, *Revolting Prostitutes: The Fight for Sex Worker's Rights* (Verso, 2020).

Maloney, Alison, 'No Woman Was Safe' (2019), retrieved from https://www.thesun.co.uk/tvandshowbiz/9120419/true-story-of-gentleman-jack-anne-lister/

Marcus, Jane, *Virginia Woolf, Cambridge and A Room of One's Own: 'The Proper Upkeep of Names'* (Cecil Woolf Publishers, 1996).

Manne, Kate, *Down Girl: The Logic of Misogyny* (Penguin, 2019).

Martin, Wednesday, *Untrue* (Scribe Publications, 2018).

Moss, Elizabeth, *Signs for Lost Children* (Granta Kindle Edition, 2015).

Mukherjee, Bharati, *Jasmine* (Virago, [1989] 1991).

Nelson, Maggie, *The Arganauts* (Mellville House, 2015).

Nin, Anaïs, *A Spy in the House of Love* (Penguin Classics, [1954] 2001).

Nin, Anaïs, *Eros Unbound* (Penguin, [1979] 2007).

Nin, Anaïs, *Henry and June* (Penguin Classics, [1987] 2017).

Parton, Dolly (1973) Jolene [Song] *Jolene*, RCA Victor.

Pinkola Estes, Clarissa, *Women Who Run with the Wolves: Myths and Stories of the Wild Woman Archetype* (Ballantine Books, 1989).

Phipps, Alison, *Me Too, Not You* (Manchester University Press, 2020).

Preciado, Paul B., *Testojunkie: Sex, Drugs and Biopolitics in the Pharmacopornographic Era* (The Feminist Press, 2013).

Preciado, Paul B., *An Apartment on Uranus*, trans. Mandell, Charlotte (Fitzcarraldo Editions, 2020).

Reader, Keith, *Intellectuals and the Left in France since 1968* (Palgrave Macmillan, 1987).

Richardson, Samuel, *Pamela: On Virtue Rewarded* (Oxford World Classics [1741] 2001).

Roche, Charlotte, *Wetlands* (Fourth Estate, 2009).

'Sex and Sexuality' Stanford Encyclopedia of Philosophy (2018), retrieved from https://plato.stanford.edu/entries/sex-sexuality/

Smart, Elizabeth, *By Grand Central Station I Sat Down and Wept* (Flamingo, [1945] 1992).

Snorton Riley, C., *Black on Both Sides: A Racial History of Trans Identity* (University of Minnesota Press, 2017).

Sollée, Kristen, *Witches, Sluts, Feminist: Conjuring the Sex Positive* (Stone Bridge Press, 2017).

Stockman, Farah, 'Monticello Is Done Avoiding Jefferson's Relationship with Sally Hemmings' (2018), retrieved from https://www.nytimes.com/2018/06/16/us/sally-hemings-exhibit-monticello.html

Story, Joseph as cited in Angert, Eugene, 'The Law Is Not a Jealous Mistress', *The Virginia Law Register, The Virginia Law Review*, 12:10 (1927), 577–93.

Sullivan, Rebecca, 'The Entire Timeline of Boris Johnson's Very, Er, Busy Romantic History', *Now to Love* (2020), retrieved from https://www.nowtolove.com.au/news/international-news/boris-johnson-wife-girlfriend-57264

Taddeo, Lisa, *Three Women* (Bloomsbury, 2019).

Taylor, Chloe, *The Routledge Guidebook to Foucault's The History of Sexuality* (Routledge, 2016).

Tinsley, Omise'eke, *Beyoncé in Formation: Remixing Black Feminism* (University of Texas Press, 2018).

Thompson, Mark et al, *Leatherfolk: Radical Sex, People, Politics and Practice* (Daedalus Publishing, 2013).

Valenti, Jessica, *The Purity Myth: How America's Obsession with Virginity Is Hurting Young Women* (Seal Press, 2010).

van der Kolk, Bessel, *The Body Keeps the Score: Mind, Brain and Body in the Transformation of Trauma* (Penguin, 2015).

Van Norden, Bryan, 'Western Philosophy Is Racist', *Aeon* (2017), https://aeon.co/essays/why-the-western-philosophical-canon-is-xenophobic-and-racist

Veaux Franklin and Rickert, Eve, *More Than Two: A Practical Guide to Ethical Polyamory* (Thorntree Press, 2014).

Walker, Alice, *The Color Purple* (Phoenix, [1982] 2017).

Walters, Joanna, 'Stormy Daniels Talks about Trump and the Worst 90 Seconds of My Life on Standup Tour', *The Guardian* (2019), https://www.theguardian.com/us-news/2019/may/08/stormy-daniels-talks-about-trump-and-the-worst-90-seconds-of-my-life-on-stand-up-tour

Watson, Christie, *The Language of Kindness: A Nurse's Story* (Vintage, 2019).

Weaver, Courtney, 'My Darling Concubine', Books, *The New York Times* (1999), retrieved from https://archive.nytimes.com/www.nytimes.com/books/99/12/05/reviews/991205.05weavert.html

Whitbread Helena, *The Secret Diaries of Miss Anne Lister Vol 1: Know My Own Heart*, ed Lister Anne (Virago, 2010).

Whitbread, Helena (ed) Lister Anne, *The Secret Diaries of Miss Anne Lister Vol 2: No Priest but Love* (Virago, 2020).

Winterson, Jeanette, *Written on the Body* (Vintage, [1992] 2001).

Woolf, Virginia, *A Room of One's Own* (Stronck Press, 2013).

Yalom, Bianca, Plovnick, Julie and Lamblin, Bianca, *A Disgraceful Affair* (Northeastern University Press, 1996).

TV/Film References

Allen, Woody (Director) (2005) *Match Point* [Film] BBC Films.

Benioff, David, Weiss, D, Strauss, Carolyn, Doelger, Frank, Caulfield, Bernadette, Cogman, Bryan, Sapochnik, Miguel and Nutter, David (Executive Producers) (2011–2019) *Game of Thrones* [TV Series] (Season 4 episode 10) HBO Entertainment, HBO.

Brand, Russell, 'WAP with Cardi B and Megan Thee Stallion: Feminist Masterpiece or Porn?' (2020), retrieved from https://www.youtube.com/watch?v=EdP9H60N2l8

Clinton, Bill, 'I Did Not Have Sexual Relations with That Woman', footage, retrieved from https://www.youtube.com/watch?v=VBe_guezGGc

Coel, Michaela, Clarke, Phil, Troni, Roberto, Miller, Sam and McLellan, Jo (executive producers) (2020) *I May Destroy You* [TV Series] Episode 8, Various Artists Limited and FALKNA Productions, BBC One, HBO.

Derrida, Jacques, On the Private Lives of Philosophers, footage, retrieved from https://www.youtube.com/watch?v=bay7Wh8D-HM

Dibb, Saul (Director) (2008) *The Duchess* [Film] Qwerty Films and Magnolia Mae Films.

Kaufman, Philip (Director) (1990) *Henry and June* [Film] Walrus and Associates.

Mundell, Claire, Kilgarriff, Elizabeth and Holmes, Gaynor (executive producers) (2018) *The Cry* [TV Series] Episode 2, Synchronicity Films, ABC, BBC One.

Origin Pictures and Cité-Amérique (2011) *The Crimson Petal and the White* [TV Series] BBC Two.

Satrapi, Marjane (Director) *Radioactive* [Film] Working Title Films and Shoebox Films.

Wilson, Ruth, Kenley-Letts, Ruth, Blair, Neil, Richer, Lucy and Eaton, Rebecca (executive producers) (2018) *Mrs Wilson* [TV Series] Snowed-In Productions, BBC One.

Legal Cases

Clinton v. Jones 520 US 681 (1997).

R v R [1991] UKHL 12.

INDEX

174INDEX